MY NAME
IS
Love

MY NAME

IS

Love

Seeing God As We've Never
Seen Him Before

TJ COLEMAN

XULON PRESS

Xulon Press
555 Winderley Pl, Suite 225
Maitland, FL 32751
407.339.4217
www.xulonpress.com

© 2024 by TJ COLEMAN

All rights reserved solely by the author. The author guarantees all contents are original and do not infringe upon the legal rights of any other person or work. No part of this book may be reproduced in any form without the permission of the author.

Due to the changing nature of the Internet, if there are any web addresses, links, or URLs included in this manuscript, these may have been altered and may no longer be accessible. The views and opinions shared in this book belong solely to the author and do not necessarily reflect those of the publisher. The publisher therefore disclaims responsibility for the views or opinions expressed within the work.

Unless otherwise indicated, Scripture quotations taken from the King James Version (KJV) – *public domain*.

Scripture quotations taken from the Holy Bible, New International Version (NIV). Copyright © 1973, 1978, 1984, 2011 by Biblica, Inc.™. Used by permission. All rights reserved.

Paperback ISBN-13: 978-1-66289-184-7
eBook ISBN-13: 978-1-66289-185-4

Contents

Opening ix

Words From a Mother. xi

Introduction. xiii

My Life Statement xv

About This Book xvii

Words From Friends xxi

Words From Kevin xxiii

Straight Wisdom From God. xxix

Chapter 1 ~ MY NAME IS LOVE 1

Chapter 2 ~ AWAKENING. 11

Chapter 3 ~ LORD & SAVIOR. 26

Chapter 4 ~ AS RELATED TO GOD 34

Chapter 5 ~ THE SIN DEBT OF ADAM 53

Chapter 6 ~ HELP US LORD. 70

Chapter 7 ~ TOOLS THROUGH THE
WISDOM OF GOD 109

Chapter 8 ~ GOD'S WOMAN 126

Chapter 9 ~ GOD'S MAN. 161

Chapter 10 ~ LIFE & DEATH FROM OUR MOUTHS. 176

Chapter 11 ~ A WILLINGNESS TO CHANGE 188

Chapter 12 ~ OUR PRIDE MUST GO 205

Decide. 228

Allow Me Lord 229

My Prayer Lord. 231

OPENING

LOVE EXPRESSES ITSELF... AS SACRIFICE

Kevin Tidwell

This book is dedicated to my brother Langston Hines. Langston was responsible for getting my first book CP TIME NO MORE published. I'll be forever grateful. You set me on my path! Thank you Bro!

Kevin Tidwell was also my brother. He was my biggest cheerleader, encouraged me, and always wanted the very best for me. My brother recently passed, and his void can not be filled. I'm grateful that his words will live on through this book. Thank you Big Bro!

WORDS FROM A MOTHER...

"It's what every Mother wants for her daughter, but don't quite know how to express it."

God has given you... Through these words!

Joi Stewart Watts

INTRODUCTION

MY NAME IS LOVE

An introduction to God as He really is. Not as we've seen Him. But in Spirit and in Truth, through the words He's given!

Imagine being a scribe for God. Imagine the things you'd hear! Imagine the wisdom, the insight, the revelation knowledge you'd receive. Imagine hearing the secrets of God.

Uncover the pages in this book that Only God Himself has given. To Help & Rescue us from ourselves! It's what's contained in the pages of this book... His Infinite, Unconditional Love For Us!

What an Incredible, Awesome... And Humbling experience!

MY LIFE STATEMENT…

I want to meet the place where my Life and Purpose intervene, and I maximize the Effectiveness and Excellence of God within me… In Service To Humanity!

tjciii

~BE WILLING TO OPEN YOUR HEART TO RECEIVE THESE TRUTHS~

"But the natural man receiveth not the things of the Spirit of God: for they are foolishness unto him: neither can he know them, because they are spiritually discerned." 1 Corinthians 2:14

GOD INTERVENES

God gives me writings that pertain to marriage. We shouldn't wait for marriage, to adapt our lives to these truths He gives; but prepare our hearts and minds today so we'll be ready, prepared and well informed. These truths will place us well ahead of where we are; of struggling and just getting by. We can be the Light & Salt God intended us to be for both Christian and worldly marriages.

The writings contained in this book can save countless marriages. It's a gift from God to us!

ABOUT THIS BOOK

CHARACTER

~ Having character is like climbing a mountain while riding a unicycle on a tightrope. It's not only the climb... It's the balance! ~

REASON & PURPOSE FOR THIS BOOK

The world is in chaos! Confusion is at its highest state. What kind of world will we leave for our children; our grandchildren and beyond! It's something we must think of now; not tomorrow. We can't place this burden on another generation. We must step forth and say... Enough!

We especially as Christian's, the called and chosen of God; must especially feel the burden and much of the responsibility for the state of the world. No, we can't save the world, but can we save our piece, our area; our part. Can we for a moment, think of someone other than ourselves; our own lives!

Part of this is our fault, as we live too close to the world. It used to be that a Christian stood out. We recognized them for their relationship with God. Today, we wear Christianity as a garment that we put on and take off depending on who we're around. This has got to change!

The world will never change unless and until it sees Light & Salt. We must show them the way, not walk amongst them and beside them in the things they're doing. We must pull them away from these things; not by our words, but by our lifestyles. Our words are the problem. We preach to them, but our lives don't align with the words we speak. So they ignore us and don't take us seriously. Who can blame them!

Christ will return one day. He's returning for His bride without spot or wrinkle. This no way resembles the church of today; not even close!

Over 30 years ago, God spoke these words to me… "I will speak to you like Moses!" I didn't know what that meant then, but I do now! God has given me a unique ability to hear His voice when He speaks to me. Early in this gift, I learned obedience to stop whatever I was doing to write down what God was saying to me. I've been doing this for 16 years now; writing whenever God speaks to me. I'm not an author; I'm a scribe of the Master. I don't pick the times, the topics or temperature in which they come. I simply write!

From the words I receive, I hear what's on the heart and mind of God. What I hear is that God has extended His patience long enough to a world gone astray. A world caught up in selfishness and me-isms. A Christian population that has abandoned our post; our duty to the world to draw and attract.

In order to draw, one must be attractive in one shape, manner or behavior. In order to be salt, one must be a seasoning in which another thirst for. Today, we're not being much of a light nor salt to a dying world in chaos and confusion. Instead, we've adopted their ways and mannerisms.

God says… It must stop! I hear Him through the words He gives me. God is not like us. He does this in love. How does He do this? He doesn't beat us over the head with a Bible. He draws, delivers and frees us with Truth, Enlightenment, Wisdom and Awareness.

ABOUT THIS BOOK

This is the reason I'm writing this book today. I couldn't sit any longer. I had to release what God has given me. God has started back to the beginning with this book. It matters not how long or how long you haven't been a Christian… We all need to take heed to these words. They're not mine! Let's make that clear upfront. I don't have such intelligence.

Where is God starting with this reconstruction of our lives? In the very place they started… The family. The dynamic of the family, which consist of the relationship of the husband and wife is where He's starting. This one dynamic effects our lives, the lives of our children, their futures and society at large.

God is saying… The Foolishness Must Stop! Come back to the light. Separate yourselves from the world. Come out from amongst them and be Light and Salt to them as is required of you.

Henceforth, the reasons and purpose for this book and every word written by the Author… God!

COMPELLED

Have you ever known something in your life that you do; but overlook. A behavior that you semi-recognize, but forget about until it happens again! Then someone puts a label; an identifier on that behavior, and you become aware of it for the rest of your life… An Awakening to Truth!

I was compelled to write and finish this book based on the subject matter given to me by God. The urgency and the need for change, prompted me to complete it and get it out to as many people as soon as possible.

MY NAME IS LOVE

I hear the urgency in the voice of God. He's preparing us for change. We have moved so far away from the ways and precepts of God. Look at society today. Trace the problems back to the lack of basic foundational principles of marriage and family. We've abandoned God's way for our own, and now our children and society are paying the bills for our neglect and selfishness.

God is giving us a chance to get things right through the words He's given. These are not parables or things hard to interpret or understand. God has given these words of wisdom, instructions, guidance and revelation knowledge in a language easily understandable to all. It's correction, guidance and admonition through love; as only God can do.

In this book, are things we didn't know to do. God is giving us different ways of seeing things; different and right ways of doing things. He's presenting Himself in ways we've not seen Him before. Not a God far off in the distance... But an ever present God, close and concerned about our lives. But we must see differently to receive. We must be willing to abandon our ways for God's.

It's then our lives, our marriages, our homes will turn around in ways we could never imagine. Take the hand of God and walk with Him in Newness of Life!

WORDS FROM FRIENDS

A GIFT FROM GOD

I understand I have a gift from God to hear His voice. It's truly an amazing privileged to hear the words God speaks. Being full of enlightenment; I need an outlet to share these beautiful words given to me by God. There are two very special people I share these writing with the most. Together we have learned, grown; and cried many tears of joy from the beauty God shares. They are the dearest of friends to me, and we've taken an amazing journey of enlightenment together.

Thank you Lucille Clark and Kevin Tidwell.

WORDS FROM KEVIN...

Psalms 147:5

> Great is our Lord, and of great power: His understanding is infinite.

Proverbs 21:30

> There is no (human) wisdom nor understanding, nor counsel against the LORD.

Psalms 146:9(b)

> ... but the way of the wicked He (God) turneth upside down.

Luke 16:15(b)

> ... for that which is highly esteemed among men is abomination in the sight of God.

I Corinthians 3:19

> ... for the wisdom of this world is foolishness with God.

Hello, friends:

The above Bible verses bring to light the sad condition of real truth in today's world culture. One has only to access most any news media, social media, or other source of information to quickly realize that the

MY NAME IS LOVE

content is conditioned, spun or otherwise conformed to whatever bias that entity supports. It's gotten to the point where I no longer refer to the purveyors of news as "news reporters," but as "news distorters!"

Sadly, this state of affairs has even metastasized from the secular into the Spiritual world. Consequently, the Good News of the Gospel is being contorted by many Good News distorters. The enemy is busy—consistently on the attack to pervert truth through the enticing misconceptions of worldly wisdom. This is why this book, "My Name is Love" by James R. Coleman III (TJ), is such a timely and essential Blessing in helping principled and honor intended people navigate through this worldly confusion.

The author, TJ Coleman is a dear and personal friend of mine. I have had the distinct honor and privilege of knowing him for more than 35 years; he is just like a brother to me. I can unequivocally declare that TJ is a deep, virtuous, genuine follower of Christ whose central life goal is to glorify God by helping others. He sincerely and earnestly has the readers' best interest at heart, and desires only to help them perceive and receive the transforming power of God's Perfect Word in their lives.

I therefore believe that the 'thinking' reader will, as I have, experience an eye opening, unique, revitalizing and personal life boost on both the Spiritual and practical levels. "My Name is Love" exposes the subtle, but dangerous fallacy of the enemy narrative and challenges the reader to up his or her game—to aim higher both internally and externally. It also stimulates us to enrich not only our own lives, but also the lives of others. The enemy doesn't want that for us, but this books punches him in the face with truth and uprightness. Amen!

Don't get it twisted… God doesn't say what is true—a statement is true because God said it! That's why the the book "My Name is Love" is so life changing; it lines up in complete accordance with the written Word. God is using TJ to elucidate and illuminate His life elevating

WORDS FROM KEVIN...

principles, so we can experience the wonderful splendor of fulfilling and purposeful living.

The book "My Name is Love" contains life empowering principles that also may help through conviction. However, don't blame the flawless mirror of truth for the image it reflects. The truths in this book are tempered with love so that conviction comes free of condemnation, accusation, criticism, or disillusionment. They say that confession is good for the soul, however, "My Name is Love" has taught me that conviction is good for personal growth. If received and applied, this book can penetrate past personal and learned bias to liberate the reader from enemy holding patterns that hinder meaningful life advancement. It can also proactively help the reader avoid life pitfalls that can be costly in resources and relationships, as well as help rectify past errors.

Lastly, just think of a homeowner reaching out to a insurance provider to initiate a policy while his house is burning!! "My Name is Love" revealed to me that this is how the enemy wants us to live out our lives; reactionary, late, lagging, always a step behind—deceived, backwards, spiritually dumbed-down, spiritually ill equipped, consistently playing catch-up and constantly existing below the high quality of life God intends for us. This book also exposed to me the world's house of distorted mirrors that the enemy wants us to remain in— where you don't know that you don't know the truth. The truth often runs counterintuitive to this world culture.

Finally, accept the transformative and personal life- challenges of this book. I think you'll find you've been missing out on much of the magnificent fulfillment available to you. I plan on using "My Name is Love" as a refresh button and as a personal revival in my life!

Thank you, TJ

WIORDS FROM LUCILLE...

The book, "My Name Is Love," is the second book written by TJ Coleman. His first book was called "CP Time No More."

I've had the pleasure of knowing TJ most of my life. He's a no nonsense kind of guy. I remember one day he told me the Lord said to him... "I will speak to you like Moses!" He described it like God's mouth to his ear.

He told me about a time when God first began to give him these writings. He thought he would be able to remember them and write them down later. But he would forget the words given to him by God. "The loss of something so precious was horrible," he said. As a result, he vowed whenever God gave him something, he would stop whatever he was doing and write it down; just as God gave it to him. He's been faithful in doing that for 16 years now.

Wait until you read these writings! You'll see that only God could be the author of these elegant insights on how to live and conduct our marriages, and everyday lives.

CP Time had me crying one moment, laughing another, and embracing at all times; the words of my savior Jesus Christ. I know without a doubt that "My Name Is Love" will do the same.

Lucille Clark

"The eyes are useless when the mind is blind." ~ Unknown

GOD IS LOVE

"God is love and whoever abides in love abides in God, and God abides in him. God is love, and all who live in love live in God, and God lives

WORDS FROM KEVIN...

in them." (1 John 4:16).His very essence is Love- a kind of love that we cannot truly comprehend because it is selfless and rejoices in truth. God's truths about love have been revealed to TJ Coleman and he has compiled it into a new book "My Name is Love."

These teachings from God, that TJ has been fortunate enough to receive, can help us follow God's plan for all our relationships. You cannot help but draw closer to God and have the opportunity to open yourself up to the word of God. You will see that these words are true, because they align with the Bible- God's love letters to us. Through these writings we learn that until we surrender to God and his infinite wisdom and love, we will fall short in our ability to love the partner that God has given us. We will fall short in our ability to love our children, who constantly test us.

We will fall short in our ability to love the neighbor and even our enemy that we have deemed unloveable. Without God at the head and center of our lives, our marriage, and our family, there will always be unfulfillment, keeping track of wrongs, and misunderstanding of why we exist in the first place.

"My Name is Love"allows God to illustrate, through His son, TJ, that our very existence is to glorify God… the design of our marriages is to glorify God. However, we can't do that if we are busy trying to steal God's light for our own. Our own disobedience to our Father dims the light. His light and His love is sufficient for our every need.

This book has helped me see that the world says our marriages and relationships should make us happy, but the creator of marriage says that we should find our strength in the joy of the Lord (Nehemiah 8:10). We no longer have to grieve or weep for what is going on around us. Downcast eyes will look for happiness which comes and goes, depending on the circumstances. Looking Heavenward, we know that joy and strength comes from the Lord's promises to us. From His love.

MY NAME IS LOVE

I pray that this book will transform your thoughts and your actions as it has mine. More than once, I had to stop reading these words and ask God for forgiveness. This book will convict all who read with an open heart and mind (and maybe some closed hearts, too) but it also leaves the reader with answers and a clear path to apply God's word. The encouragement and guidance I have received from this book is immeasurable, just like God's love.

Let your heart be shaped by the One who created it. Let God's love wash over you. "Let all that you do be done in love." (1 Corinthians 16:14).

If you do not know the saving grace of Jesus Christ or have a relationship with our Father God, you can start to learn about God through this book "My Name is Love." If you already have surrendered your messy, imperfect, selfish ways to Him, then this book will help deepen your relationship as you hear from God in new ways in "My Name is Love."

Oh by the way— James Coleman (TJ) happens to be my cousin. We were never close growing up and I barely knew him. Our grandmother's were sisters. We were living separate lives with a "hey cousin" whenever we would run into each other. Then one day TJ told me about a special project he was working on. It turns out it was to shine light on and encourage/grow the young teens in our hometown. He expanded that into a program for younger school age children who were missing a father figure. He has totally and thoroughly touched the lives of nearly everyone in this community.

I've seen firsthand the impact His love has had on everything through the obedient heart of TJ. He has understood the Father's love for a long long time and I believe that is why God chose him to reveal these profound thoughts in "My Name is Love."

Debra D 'Attoma

STRAIGHT WISDOM FROM GOD...

IT WASN'T HER THAT CHANGED... IT WAS ME!

This wasn't about her. It was about me. More specifically, it was between me and God!

I wanted her to change. I needed her to change. But who did God produce change in... Me! God began with getting my attention. Then He made room to place His desire within me.

I went from thinking what I wanted to do, to desiring what He wanted me to do and be. It's not that God was so persuasive, it's that I've given Him room to deposit His desires within my heart as He pleases.

They then become the things I want and move towards. This is the fulfillment of the scripture in action when it says... "Take delight in the LORD, and he will give you the desires of your heart." Psalms 37:4

God wasn't saying that He was giving us everything we desired. He was saying there would come a time in our walk with Him through maturity, that we would surrender our will to allow God to exchange His desires for ours. And those desires would become the very things we want most.

I now saw her unlike any time before. She was my desire. I saw my place and purpose as man and husband in her life. Not as chore, but as privilege. I put away my pride and became expressive with my words towards her. In every way, my desire was to please her, to support her; to cover her in love and care.

This is not always who I was. I tried to be. But this was different. I was no longer doing this within the limits of my finite strength. I was now doing it in the limitless strength and wisdom of God without walls or boundaries… Without Pride! I now saw things with a laser focus. The Bible says… "As a man thinks in his heart, so is he." Proverbs 23:7 It was true!

By allowing God to place the desire in my heart to be this man; this husband… I desired to become him. I purposed in my heart through my thoughts; this is who I was! My body, my energy, my mind; moved me towards being this man.

Soon, I became so focused on the change in myself; more than her. This was no longer about her. It was about me and my relationship with God. I wanted to please Him more than anything!

This was a partnership in purpose. Maybe He used the leverage of my love for her to change me. It no longer mattered to me. What mattered was my obedience to God. Regardless of her… This is who He needed me to be for Him and purpose.

Could I have chosen the time of my metamorphosis! Maybe; maybe not! I'm just thankful that it came. No matter the time; the change came when I surrendered and released my will to God. God, in His infinite sovereignty knew the day of my arrival.

Want change in your spouse! Allow God to drop His desires for you in your heart. You'll no longer be focusing on your spouse. Your attention will be on the new person God placed inside of you.

Chapter 1

MY NAME IS LOVE

I called my Mom to read her something without explaining what it was or what it was about. I read to her… My Name Is Love.

She said… "THAT SOUNDS LIKE GOD!" It is Him Mom. It is Him!

REVERENCE FOR ALMIGHTY

Rarely do I get a writing from God about Himself. This one took me a few days, as I was extremely hesitant about the words. Although these words were given to me, I read them over and over again.

I didn't feel worthy to write them, or even receive them. The majority of the writings I receive from God are about us. Those I learn from! Those have changed my life. This one was different!

I was hesitant to even share them with anyone! This was God! The Most High Himself! He was giving me words in our day, in our language to describe Himself.

As long as I've been His scribe, and write what He gives me; this one I didn't feel worthy to hear or to pen. It brings tears to my eyes even now just writing about it.

MY NAME IS LOVE

I see God differently now. All those years of being groomed and sharpened; all those years in the wilderness crying out for release... I saw Him as a taskmaster. It was all worth it of course. From it, I received two incredible gifts... The gifts of Brokenness & Humility!

Now I see Him as the Loving Father He is. He is love. The source of love. Love isn't what I always thought it was. I was way off base. I apologize!

When I shared these words with a few people close to me, I never heard such responses from any other writing.

This was God Himself. His name is Love! He was coming down to our level; our language and revealing Himself like we've never saw Him before. He would convict us in love as only He could do. The people that I shared these words with... Wanted To Change; when they heard them! I've never seen anything like it in my life. They were hungry; looking forward to hearing these words To Change! Only God could do this!

MY NAME IS LOVE

Hello... My name is Love. You may know me by other names. I am known by many.

I am the wind; the Sun and the stars. I am Heaven and Earth. I am All things.

Designer, Architect, Engineer... Creator of life and all its inhabitants. I am All Sufficient!

I am Perfect. Without Fault. I am without limit or measure. Lacking nothing! I'm Inexhaustible!

MY NAME IS LOVE

I am Always. I am Ever. I have no start. I have no end. I surpass time and existence. I will always Be!

Time is your measuring stick; not Mine. I'm unrestricted; to time, space and distance. I encompass all!

My name is Love! I would like to introduce Myself to you, and reintroduced Myself to others.

Do you know me? Or only think you know me. I may not be as you thought. Not of this world; My ways may not be as you think.

You can not conjure who I am. I Am! You can not modify who I am. I Am! You can not have your own version of Me. I am Genuine; Original… And can not be duplicated!

You must come to me, in Truth to know me. I can not be found elsewhere.

I am free! I am the Essence of life! I am Innocence; like the heart of a child.

Beauty is My expression.

I am gentle. I am kind. I am Strength. I hold all power of the Universe.

I am Light! See me. Be drawn to me. I am your path out of darkness.

If you know Me, you know that I am Peace. I am Joy. I am Wisdom. All that's good… I am!

I am Care. I am Compassion. I am Expression!

My nature is giving. My bounty is ever my delight. My supply is endless. My resources sure!

MY NAME IS LOVE

Know me; not of Me. Seek Me, and you will find. Serve Me in freedom; without chore. My ways are easy, yet require restraint, discipline; and commitment.

Eat of Me in abundance. Thirst of my nectar; without measure. My fruits are endless.

At times, you have misspoken of me. I couldn't do such things; be such things. I am Sure! Without change; I am constant, reliable; dependable.

I am boundless. I have no limits. Like the wind; I can not be contained. I am Infinite. I can't be measured.

I am Character! I gave birth to Integrity and Truth.

Only I am Complete! I am Whole! I am Absolute!

My Name Is Love!

> "I have never heard anything like that in my life. It's one of the most beautiful thing I've ever heard! That's transcendent. That's on another level. That's definitely from God telling you who He is!"

> Kevin Tidwell

> "Wow! You truly are hearing from God; unquestionable! It bowls me over. It met me right where I am!"

> Debra D'Attoma

MY NAME IS LOVE

THE DISCIPLINE OF LOVE

Through the wisdom of God, I see the depths of love. I understand it more clearly than ever before. I see love beyond my feelings. I see that it's so much more. I see that there's a discipline to love.

Love is giving, and it triggers our emotions. But for the first time I'm seeing a different side of love that was always there. It was unspoken. It was not labeled until now in my mind to readily identify. It's the restraints through love.

Yes, we're taught all of our lives that to love we must give something. We must give our hearts, display our feelings and release our emotions. But once we find love through the life of another individual through covenant or marriage; love also comes with disciplines.

What this means is there are things we give, and there are things we don't give because of love. We give our commitment to the One we marry. Through this love, and because of this love; what we give to them and how we relate to them is like none other.

We withhold that part of our love, specifically and only for them. This is the type of love we demonstrate through our bodies. This is love in the realm of marriage. This is love given and reserved for only one. This is the discipline of love. It requires restraint through commitment and dedication.

I also see another type of love. Before, I've mainly only seen love one way. I've seen it primarily based on my emotions; touchy-feeling only.

Now I see the love of God through discipline and correction too. Because God loves us, He corrects us. He sets us on our proper paths through correcting us. This is not always a pleasant thing, and sometimes comes with consequences to prevent us from repeating our mistakes. It's no different than us as parents correcting; teaching our children through the discipline of love. The Bible tells us… "For the LORD disciplines those He loves, and He punishes each one He accepts as his child." Hebrew 12:6

Love has many faces. It shows through our emotions, through acts and behaviors. It's displayed through restraint, through withholding; through commitment for our spouses. It's displayed through discipline, and corrected through punishment by God; and us as parents.

Thank you Lord for the expansion of my mind through understanding and revealing that love doesn't just have one face as I've always believed.

Love has many faces!

I APOLOGIZE

Love is Intensity. You go after it. You go get it. You run to it. You display it.

Love is Energy. You have it. You give it. You demonstrate it. You pass it on.

Love is Passion. You release it. You feel it. You pursue it… You dream it!

Love is not task orientated. It's not based on what I do for you. It's not generated or predicated on objects or deeds. You love me because I do this for you, or I buy that for you. No! Love is! Love me for who I am!

When I got married, I married for love. I knew no different. I married my wife because I loved her and wanted to spend my life with her. But through spiritual maturity, I've changed. My marriage is no longer about me loving my wife. It's about me loving God!

MY NAME IS LOVE

Because I love God, I lay down my life for her, and love her as Christ loved the church. Because I love God, my pride and ego has been pushed aside to meet her needs and the needs of our family.

Because I love God, I see her differently. I see her as a gift. I act differently towards her. Without chore or effort, I express my appreciation for her, my need for her unashamed, and my desire… Only for her!

Loving God gives us focus. It removes foolishness and trinkets from our vision, from our pathways and desires. We see things with purity and light.

I love the group Incognito. They give me something in their music. But is that really love just because they give me something! Is love only in reception! What about those I obtain nothing from. Do I not love them for the lack of receipt?

Or is love my attitude towards the world and others. Is love the foundation of who I decided; who I chose to be by adopting the principles of God as the primary characteristics in my life… Being patient and kind. Not being proud, boastful and selfish.

There are those I will never meet or know. Are not All my neighbors according to the Bible. Neighborhood has little to do with proximity in the sight of God, but everything to do with the equality of love for humanity.

I've come to an understanding… Love is not just my feelings. It's my behavior. Its my attitude. My altitude. It's my restraint. It's not just my emotions. It's my control over them. It's my barometer to measure alignment.

It's not even what I have in abundance or lack for you. It's who I'm willing, and have chosen to be for God and myself.

MY NAME IS LOVE

I am this regardless of you. I have adopted these precepts of God as content within my character. I've solidified them as foundational principles in my heart.

So love is not the product of my feelings, but the expression of them! Love is not the sum of my emotions, but the control of them!

All of my life... I've been misled!

I now see that love has little to do with my feelings and more to do with my choice. How do I have feelings for those I don't know. Of course I don't have the same feelings for them as my children, family and friends; yet I'm still required to have love for them.

I now see that it's my disposition, it's my decision to live my life being kind and wanting the best for others. My feelings are not even part of this equation. I do simply because I am; because I've decided to exhibit the fruits of love through my personality and behavior. My desire to do good for others will be exhibited through my expression.

We have associated love completely and explicitly with our feelings. Unfortunately, we have been misled, misguided and misinformed. Love is what we do. Love is what we demonstrate through patience, kindness; selflessness.

If Love was an arrow, the characteristics would be the tip of the arrow. The demonstration of love would be the shaft. And the very end; the tail of the arrow; would be the expression of love... Our feelings!

We've been shooting our arrows backwards!

These words God has given me have taken the pressure off of love for me through awareness; through understanding. Love is not what

I thought it was. All of my life, I've primarily been loving with my feelings. There was always so much more to love.

Love... I apologize!

I PRAY LORD

I pray Lord that Your Wisdom would be with me in simplicity, in complexity; in truth. I pray that She would give me the ability to see, to know and to do. Also when, how and why.

I pray that Understanding would forever assist Her and give me comprehension, clarity, insight and the ability to grasp the many ways and avenues that Wisdom flows.

She's beautiful Lord! She's the beauty in all things seen and unseen. She's the beauty in the flower, the majesty in the mountain, the might in the sea. She is delicate and strength. She encompasses it all!

There is none like Her. She's forever Your glory, beholding Your Magnificent wonders. I pray that She would forever abide with me Lord and that She would reflect all of the beauty that is You through works and efforts in my life.

Show Her to the world Lord! Put Her on display for mankind to behold; and never to deny. May She bend the hearts of humanity back towards You, with signs and wonders unspeakable; unseen an unimagined.

May She point an arrow straight back to You Lord as the Source of all of Her fascination, that mankind would fall on our knees in Humility, Reverence and Honor, which is so befitting to You!

MY NAME IS LOVE

Wisdom… show me God, my Father and all His Wondrous works displayed.

From Kevin…

> TJ, this writing not only earnestly and meticulously personified Love to me, but revealed the true Glory, Majesty & Splendor of God's Love! It amazes me that Almighty God continues to reveal more aspects of Himself through His Chosen Vessels, of which you are certainly one!
>
> K

Chapter 2

AWAKENING

~I WOKE UP... AND FOUND MYSELF ASLEEP!~

The thing about being Asleep is... You don't realize it until you've been Awakened!

IT'S A SHAME... WE AS PEOPLE, SEE THE IMMENSE VALUE IN SOMETHING OR SOMEONE, ONLY AFTER WE'VE LOOKED BACK THROUGH THE EYES OF TIME, OR THROUGH THE PAIN OF LOSS!

WE MUST LEARN TO GRASP VALUE WHILE IT STANDS WITHIN OUR IMMEDIATE PRESENCE... THROUGH THE FORTUNE OF WISDOM!

A man once said... "He who looks outside of himself dreams. But he who looks within... AWAKENS"

DECLARATION OF A NEW DAY!

I would like every couple to speak this New Day Declaration out loud to each other. Afterwards, there's no going back to old ways, habits; mannerisms that have been unproductive in your marriage.

MY NAME IS LOVE

No more following the world, what's cool and what people are doing on TV. You will only move forward by letting go of the past; forgiving and repositioning yourselves back in your original place before God... Submitting yourselves, and your will for the plans and purpose God has for your marriage, family and lives.

A NEW DAY DECLARATION...

I apologize for who I've been and for what I've done.

Please forgive me!

I have not seen you as I should have.

As a gift from God.

As of this day; that will change!

I'm asking God to show me how to love you!

You are not my enemy!

And I'm not yours!

God called us to be One in Life & Purpose through marriage.

I'm willing to forgive, and put the past behind us.

I'll not bring up toxic wounds and conversations again.

What's dead is dead!

And we'll not dig it up!

We're walking in the light of God!

I Surrender selfishness, pride, anger; stubbornness.

I've done it my way long enough!

I Surrender!

God has assigned purpose for our marriage.

Lord, I surrender to Your plans for our marriage, for our children; for our family.

IT'S A NEW DAY!

IJNAM

AWAKEN

Awaken from your slumber. Arise from your shadow, and come into the light.

Be shaken from slumber to awareness. From darkness to consciousness. From blindness to enlightenment.

O man asleep... Arise!

You are such; more than you see.

You have much; more than you know.

You contain vast treasures within.

Dormant and hidden.

Discover your truth!

Step into your light.

Become aware of your greatness.

Behold your magnificence.

Slumber no more!

AWAKENING

Each day the dawn awakens. It brings with it... The new day! Light appears, and has vanquished the dark. It has conquered once again in the cycle put in place by the Law of the Almighty.

"Let there be Light!" Genesis 1:3 And it was so, and it's still so, since those words burst through nothingness and overpowered the void of darkness.

Light had entered the world! Illumination had taken aim on the sight of existence. Clarity was brought forth. Now I see with vibrancy. Now I behold the wonders of His words fashioned into being. It wasn't His hands that built; that created... It was simply His words!

Words released in the expanse of nothingness; in obedience, to shape and form into existence... Crossing over into life!

Each day confirms the fact that all things obey God. Told only once, it walks in true alignment and obedience to its Creator. That cycle of obedience, called a Law of God and the Universe, awakens us to light each day.

The cycle of God continues!

AWAKENING

THE LADY IN THE AISLE

Words in a binder, I would carry around. Words from God given to me. I would go around and ask pastors if I could share them with their congregations.

They weren't my words… They were God's!

The words weren't just for me. They were for all of us. I simply wrote them down as they were given to me by God. It was a gift; and part of my purpose from Him.

What a privilege to hear these words God would speak to me. I hadn't asked for this, it was given. But I learned early, that it was an honor to hear, to write; to share what I've been given of God.

I realized quickly, these words weren't just for me. Everyone needed to hear them. They would help us all. So I gathered some of them together in a binder. I would share them with pastors and ask if I could share some of the words with their congregations. No response! No invitations!

One pastor told me to come to his church to one of his services. I went. During the service, he came down from the pulpit and stood on the first pew in the church. I looked around to see what everyone else was thinking. Was this a normal occurrence!

During the offering I approached the pastor and asked him if I could share one of the writings given to me by God. He gave me permission to share.

I stood in front of the church, and read just one

of the writings, word for word just as given to me by God. I never talk over the writings God gives me. I read them just as they're given.

MY NAME IS LOVE

I read the writing. I began walking back to my seat down the aisle. Suddenly, a young lady got out of her seat, and met me in the aisle. Her words to me were… "Can I have a copy of that!" I said sure, you can have this one!

She was looking for substance. She was looking for truth. She needed something from God.

I learned something that day that I will never forget. This is what God showed me… SOMETIMES WE TRY TO MANUFACTURE SUBSTANCE RATHER THAN BEING A CHANNEL FOR ITS RELEASE!

I never did understand the thing about the pew. I do know as a minister myself; I have seen people do things to try to get the congregation fired up. I'm not into that!

I went up there, read what was given to me by God; added nothing extra to it… And went to take my seat! It were those words, God given; with substance, that moved that young lady from her seat. She didn't wait until after church to approach me. In spite of any embarrassment or shame; she moved out of her seat. In spite of peer pressure or any such thing; she was there waiting for me in the aisle; needing what I had in my hand from God.

It's a dying world! Are we really helping people with performance in church! People are crying out for help; for truth! The young lady in the aisle didn't wait. Those words given to me by God spoke to her heart and she needed them. Those words compelled her to get out of her seat to ask for a copy. Not my words; the words given to me of God.

There are so many words God has given me to set us free, to enlighten and save us from ourselves. I decided to quit begging pastors to allow me to share these words. Instead, I prayed for God to give me a platform in which to share them. They're His words. I'm just His scribe. I write as the Master speaks. I pick neither the words, subjects or the times given. I know my place and I know God's. He's Master and I'm servant.

For now, I will use the platform of this book to share the words given to me by God. I will let Him do the multiplying.

These words will touch our hearts; free us and awaken us to truth... Just like the Lady in the Aisle!

UNORTHODOX

As I've grown spiritually my desires have changed. I've been taken back to school by God. I've been re-educated!

I've been given new eyes, new direction; new vision. I can see the stars and beyond. There's been an replacement of my old selfish desires, for new desires that God Himself has placed within my heart. It's a freedom I've never known or experienced.

I thought I would be losing by giving up the things I wanted most. I found that I would have those things, and even more than I could ever imagine.

The ways of God are strange to the natural mind; foolish actually. It's why few follow them; because 1+1=9 in God's language. It doesn't equate to what we've been taught all of our lives. Therefore, to receive the things we've been praying for, and the things we ask of God... We must understand His language and formulas. Not our own! This is why we miss out and our prayers are elusive.

We've been applying our own logic with spiritual formulas. We'll never solve spiritual problems with earthly logic.

MY NAME IS LOVE

All of our lives we've been trying to get something natural from something natural. Now that we are in Christ, our lives require us to get something spiritual from Someone spiritual. This will not work with our old ways of thinking.

The ways of God are as an oxymoron to us. They're foolish to the wise. This tells us that we mustn't hold on to what we've been taught all of our lives after we come to God, because those ideas and philosophies won't work.

To receive from God, we must eliminate our old ways and thoughts of reception. We must be willing to walk in the unorthodox. We must be willing to stretch our minds and do things that will not make sense to our natural minds. This is a spiritual thing! This is in God's realm. It's a place most of us have never been. How can we think what we use naturally will work with The Most High! We must come to His terms and His ways for our reception.

First, we must believe what He says, no matter how strange it meets our minds. Secondly, we must know and meet the conditions of the scripture, in order to qualify for its promises. Thirdly, we must act on His word by doing whatever it tells us, no matter how foolish it seems to us.

I'd rather receive the foolish things of God than the natural things of man. The foolish things of God come with miracles, open doors, revelation knowledge and answered prayers. They may also come with requirements that won't make sense. Do them anyways!

Walk around the walls nine times and on the tenth time shout. Don't use force or fighting. God's ways work through obedience; not sacrifice. Then watch the walls come down!

Having trouble in your marriage? Do what God requires instead of your ways, thoughts and philosophies. Ignore your negative friends and the

AWAKENING

world, and do what God says instead. It will go against your natural instincts. It will pull and stretch you in a new direction.

Submit yourself to your spouse, and watch freedom come like you've never experienced it. Watch and see that you'll actually love it; and find it refreshing. You'll find It wasn't the burden you've always thought it would be. Plus, you'll begin to live your life and marriage like you've never had before. You'll experience the residuals of your obedience through the new person your spouse has become; now that you've aligned yourself with the principles of God.

Want to help your husband be a greater man! Line up with the principles of God! Our problem is that we expect results from little or no effort. Obedience x The Principles of God = Success. This is God's formula for life more abundantly in every aspect of our lives.

Unfortunately, we've been using our own formula of… Wishing/Hoping + Minimal Effort = Little/Sporadic Results!

The Bible says… "Husbands, love your wives as Christ loved the church and gave Himself up for it." Ephesians 5:25 Put your pride aside. Forget what the guys at work think. Forget what anyone thinks! Then watch the difference in your wife. Watch the difference in the ways she sees you; the way she responds to you. She was just waiting to feel safe in your leading. She was waiting to feel secure in your love and intentions towards her. She was waiting to see that she could follow you as you follow God. It's what any woman desires most.

If God places something on your heart to do… Do it! Test the spirit to know that it's from God. Know that it's not going to harm anyone and that's it's good for someone. It will require faith on your part. It will require you to step out of your comfort zone; to look different, to act differently. But the results will be incredible. And on top of that, you'll gain confidence and increase your faith to do what God ask of you the next time. This is called Spiritual Growth!

Today is a new day in your walk and relationship with God. It's a new day for your marriage and life; now that you've properly learned the ways of God more clearly.

Put away your old thoughts and ways, and adopt and accept the unorthodox of God!

You have to give up to gain. You have to released to receive. You have to die to self to live.

These are the ways; the unorthodox ways of God!

We've been trying to put our square ways into His round hole requirements! I just doesn't work!

IT WASN'T YOU

It was their sideways agenda. The greatest thing on Earth is love. It's who God is. It's His nature. His love is boundless, without limits; incomprehensible! We can never fully understand it nor measure it accurately.

With such a beautiful gift, the enemy would have a fake to draw us and trick us into believing what we think is love. He's the father of lies and tries to counterfeit the authenticity of God by making a similarity of the good God created.

God created love. The love of God is natural and pure. Lust is thinly veiled, and can appear and be mistaken for love. Only the wise and discerning will know the difference. One can bring tremendous joy; the other, tremendous heartache and damage. One is wrapped in truth.

AWAKENING

One disguised in lies! One is selfless and giving. One only takes; to ruin. One seeks the betterment of us. One seeks its own agenda.

With such disparities, then how are we tricked and fooled into falling and believing in such individuals to the point of having relationships with them and even marrying them? The truth is… People lie! How did you know they were lying--Their lips were moving!

The truth is, people successfully appear to be someone they aren't until they get what they want. Then the truth really comes out. The false face falls off, and for the first time; we see the true image of the individual we've invested time, effort and love in. It was love on your part… A lie on theirs!

Two or three children later, a divorce, financial and emotional ruin; you're devastated and if you're a Christian… Blaming God! But God told us in His word before we did this… "Can one take fire into their blossom and not be burned?" Proverbs 6:27 But he was so fine! She had a body for days! I'm attracted to bad boys! All of it as Solomon said "Is vanity!"

It's emptiness in the end, and such a person leaves us in the recovery room of life, hoping and praying that we can move on from the wake of their devastation. The truth is, we can not afford to go through such things any longer. Time is short and we must be in the settle down phases of our lives; preparing for the return of Christ. We can ill afford to keep jumping from one bad relationship to the next. It's time we do as the Bible tells us, and only partner with someone, not that says they're a Christian; but with someone that demonstrates they have a relationship with Christ! We must "Yoke" ourselves equally with someone with similar spiritual intentions. Which means someone that has accepted Christ as their personal Savior, and they have a relationship with Him. The goal is to partner with someone who loves God more than us. This person's commitment and obligation to God will filter down into a sincere love for us.

Later for those days of people saying I'm a Christian! Anyone can say that. Where the rubber meets the road is their lifestyle. Christianity is not like a garment that we put on and take off at our leisure. It's one we wear all the days of the week, and even when no one is watching us. It's a lifestyle we're committed to; not a religion!

These days are not the days to be single in a world of darkness. A world who could care less about you, and would seek only what they can get from you, and move on to the next victim! We must screen anyone that attempts to come into our jurisdiction by asking the hard and tough questions. Like… Do you have a relationship with Christ? How do you feel about relationships/marriage? Do you like kids? Could you accept my children? How are you when you get angry? How are you financially? Do you have a job; your own place or do you still live with your mom? What's your plans for the next five years; ten years? Do you know your gift; your purpose from God. Are you walking in it?

Too many of us have been scorned; left broken, used and damaged. Some of us knew that person wasn't good for us in the beginning, but we took them in anyways. They left damage in their wake. We can't keep bouncing back. We're damaged goods for the right and real person God would give us. We push them away from the damage left by the wrong one. We miss out!

Time is winding up. The enemy seeks to ruin us through our hearts, and that comes through our poor choices through relationships. It leaves us with children; broken homes, scratching our heads wondering what just happened.

For the beauty of love that God has, and all the fruit that comes with it, the enemy has a fake; sick and twisted. The love of God edifies. What the enemy provides tears down, diminishes, demolishes and destroys.

God gave us a measuring stick to recognize love in the Bible. We must use it as wisdom in anything, and anyone that comes into our space. The Bible tells us that… "Love is patient, love is kind. It does not envy, it does not boast, it is not proud. It is not rude, it is not self-seeking, it is not easily angered, it keeps no record of wrongs. Love does not delight in evil but rejoices with the truth." 1 Corithians 13:4-8

If a person isn't demonstrating these qualities consistently to you and they're telling you they love you; you're falling for the fake; thinly veiled substitute by the enemy. Know the truth! Measure it by the one and only definition of love given to us by God.

NO ROOM

God and I came to an agreement several years ago. That agreement was, for any awards, recognitions, applause or accomplishments that I obtained in life, I will gladly give Him the recognition for them.

One day God informed me that I was required to go to school. It wasn't a normal school with normal teachers. It was a huge building full of rooms.

I quickly noticed that this school was much different than the schools I previously attended. Instead of going into classes, I learned my lessons outside of them.

My instructor was stern. He took his job very seriously as if my outcome would have a huge impact on something. He kept me in line and focused.

MY NAME IS LOVE

You see, every time I went to enter a room in this school, I was told the very same thing… No Room, No Room!

No matter what door I approached with my instructor, his response was always the same to me… No Room, No Room!

Upon my graduation, I received a diploma; although my feet had never crossed the threshold of any room.

As I exited the building upon my graduation, I turned back to see the name of this unusual school. The words in big letters said… "SCHOOL OF HUMILITY!"

It was only clear to me then why my instructor hadn't allowed me in any of the rooms. One room there was full of pride. One was full of arrogance. One was full of those wanting power, and the ability to control the lives of others. One room was full of praise, recognition, attention and applause. Now that room was exciting! People were standing to their feet clapping, applauding and lifting individuals up. Yet this or none of these rooms, was I allowed.

My instructor finally said to me, you were chosen to attend this school for a purpose. Because of your assignment from God and the promise that you made to Him, you needed to attend this unusual school.

The rooms that you saw full of people were others in life that God had also given gifts to. But somehow along their paths, they became distracted and ended up in the rooms you saw with pride, arrogance, power, control and the rooms which praised, applauded and lifted them up.

Although you have been given a gift, the gift you have belongs to God. It's why when you went to the rooms with pride and arrogance, you were turned away because the gift deposited from God upon you; leaves No Room for you to Boast.

AWAKENING

When you attempted to enter the room to obtain power and control over others, the gift God placed within you is actually for the benefit of others and not yourself, so the highest rank you could ever obtain in the service of God is Servant. That's why you were turned back from entering that room, because there was No Room for the desire to control others as a Servant of God.

The reason you weren't allowed in the room where all the praise, applause and recognition was going on, was because the gift you have is God's. The ability to use it is God's, and the ability to influence others within it and through it is also God's. So that my son; left you with nothing worthy of praise, recognition or applause. You too were turned away from that room.

You have received your diploma because you accepted and acknowledged your place in the service of God. You have obtained the highest achievement this school could ever bestow... The service of God, towards all people, with a gift from God, to acknowledge God.

That Left No Room For You!

Chapter 3

LORD & SAVIOR

"Whoever desires among you to be great, let him be your Servant." Matthew 20:26

LORD AND SAVIOR

How do we know Jesus? What's our Christian experience. Do we relate to Him, or have a relationship with Him. There is a difference!

Through our Christian experience we come to Christ. Salvation is free. But it doesn't stop there. This is only where it begins.

When we accept Christ, we accept Him as He is… He is both Lord and Savior! He saved us from living lives of sin. He saves us from eternal separation from God once we leave this life.

This is just the beginning of our relationship with Christ. There's a place in our walk with Him that we must allow Him to be Lord of our lives also. Some of us are… Stuck At Salvation!

We confessed Jesus and accepted Him in our hearts, but our lives haven't changed much at all. We can go to church every Sunday and read the Bible everyday; but there still must be a time when we allow Jesus to be Lord of our lives.

LORD & SAVIOR

What does this mean? This is the place where we no longer hold on to our will and our lives. This is the place where we surrender these things to Christ.

Some of us fear this place because we believe we're giving up too much of ourselves; too much control of our lives. We still want to be at the helm; doing what we want to do. We're afraid of losing our lives. The truth is... This is where we truly begin to live them!

We don't know what's best for us. We only think we know. Living in the world showed us our need for God. We realized there must be a better way of doing things than the way we were living.

God led us to Him through salvation. But salvation only gets us in the door. We've surrendered only a part of us. There's more!

What can a Christian life look like at this stage. It can be a person that says they're a Christian, but there's little evidence. We can still be in the in between phase of wanting Christ, and parts of our old life, with the temptations of the world. Because we haven't taken that final step, we bear little or no fruit in our lives. Our witness to others is watered down because the people around us see no difference in our lives. We look no different. We say we're one thing, yet live another life entirely. Christianity at this place is something we put on and off like a garment, depending on which situation and people we find ourselves.

Our lives; nor our lifestyles, have changed much. And they won't until we surrender them to Christ. A life surrendered to Christ will take on a completely different look, outlook and effectiveness.

Once we surrender, we give God permission to make us the person we were always meant to be. God is a gentleman and will not force us to do anything. We must be willing. We must give Him permission by our surrender.

We'll live the lives He intended us to live. We'll no longer stand in the middle and look both ways. Our lives take on new meaning and new direction. We're serious with God now, and we allow Him to change us for the better.

Obedience, sacrifice, selflessness come into our lives now as priorities. Life is no longer about us. We can look back and see who we were. We can see clearly now through the fog and haze. We confess before God that we no longer want to be this person. We desire change in our lives and we're serious about it.

Our lives are no longer lived for ourselves. Now we understand the reason for our living… To effectively live our lives through Christ, that He can be a witness; light and salt to others.

Now others take notice of us. Now they can see the difference in us. The ways and things we used to do; the desire has fallen off. Our desire now is to please God in every phase of our lives.

We have kneeled before God and given Him permission to make our lives beautiful and effective. As the Bible says… "Old things are passed away, behold all things are become new!" 2 Corinthians 5:17

Salvation is very important. But it's just the beginning of our walks with God. It's when we allow Him to be Lord of our lives that we really change and begin to take on new lives. And the world will know we're serious; from the fruit of the lifestyles that we bear!

One day I got saved; to keep from going to Hell. One day I surrendered in my salvation to allow Jesus to be Lord over my life. There must be two surrenders in our walks with Christ. That was the day I truly began to live!

THE HAND, THE FACE; THE MOUTH OF GOD

I've noticed a transition in my walk and relationship with God. This is not something I learned overnight, but through years.

My walk with Christ has not moved in a straight line. There's been walk-towards… And walk-away from; due to sheer disappointments. At times I've lost trust. At times I've lost faith.

But the hardest part of all was the wilderness. It was a place no matter how hard I tried, I only moved so far. It was exhausting, and went on for years. I knew God had a plan and purpose for my life; but no matter what I did to go forward… I remained!

It wasn't just that! For the first time in my life, I found myself alone. And to add to it; I was now100% disabled and in constant, terrible pain in my life; with severe depression due to the pain. It was a recipe for disaster.

The thing about it; I knew I was in the wilderness. I was use to being successful in my life before. So I knew the difference. I worked hard to push myself; and excelled at whatever I did. Now nothing! I was confused… Tired; frustrated! Many times I just thought about checking out of life. But like Joseph; God had spoken incredible words over my life at a young age. It's the one light of hope I had.

This went on for 10 years! So many times I prayed and asked; begged, God to turn it off. Please God… I'm tired, was my constant cry! My tears did not move God to remove me from the wilderness!

As I now look back through those years, I followed the Voice of God to start The Aubrey Stewart Project. A man from my hometown, I never knew; but a war hero nonetheless.

MY NAME IS LOVE

I said I followed the Voice of God to do this. That voice came only with general instructions and a theme… Start this and do it for these reasons was the sum of it. I had no idea what I was doing. I made mistakes. I taxed people's time by speaking too long during my programs; speaking about the wrong things. Now I can look back on all of that 16 years later and see a successful, respected program for Mr. Aubrey, for children and adults. By my mistakes, I learned invaluable lessons on how to refine myself, my program and what I did for God. Through my mistakes, I learned the privilege of having an audience. Within that privilege, you say what you have to say… Then you take your seat! You're very respectful of people's time; even in the purpose of God.

Through the wilderness, I acted on my faith and did what God asked of me. It wasn't easy; but look at all the lives God is touching through this project today! Absolutely incredible!

The wilderness is not a pretty place. It's the place the chosen of God go to be trained. It's mandatory; not voluntary! It's the place you get to know the mouth of God for the work He'll have you doing later! It's the place you'll be rid of something we all need taken from us; Pride, and replaced with something we all need… Humility!

I can see through life and my relationship with God, the different phases. I called it… Who I saw God as, and what I wanted most from Him.

In the beginning, and the majority of my walk with God; I sought His hand! What can God give me! What can He do for me! My prayers centered around asking God to give me something, to do something in my life or to rescue me from me from some situation. It's all I knew!

Over time I grew in my relationship with Him and I began to seek His face. Now, it just wasn't what I wanted from Him; but who He is… The person of God!

LORD & SAVIOR

With this came a deepened relationship through gratitude and appreciation. I wasn't always asking God for things; material things or frivolous things. Now I asked Him for tools to help me fulfill my purpose on Earth, and in the lives of others. I was asking to help build his Kingdom on Earth while I lived. My concept of God changed; which changed my prayers.

This last phase of my life goes back to the wilderness phase of my life; when I would one day seek the Mouth of God for instructions, guidance, revelation knowledge and wisdom for the purpose assigned to my life. This very writing is a testament to that.

God gives me words, sentences and paragraphs; which turn in to these writings... Which by faith; turn into books. I depend upon the Mouth of God to direct and guide me in my projects, in doing for and recognizing others. As a result; I've seen some fascinating and incredible ways that God touches the lives of others by doing what He tells me to do. So many times, I am unashamedly moved to tears at the sheer beauty that I see and experience.

The Hand, the Face; the Mouth of God... Now that you know, you can ask yourself; where are you in your walk with Him.

I will say this in my closing... The wilderness was the most difficult time in my life. It was the most necessary time in my life. Through it, God gives the most beautiful and incredible gift, that we don't obtain without suffering. That irreplaceable and most important gift in the service of God; wasn't His anointing... It was Humility. Without humility; how can any of us truly walk in the anointing of God. It's something we neglect to understand.

The gifts of God aren't given to puff us up... But to lift Him up! Only humility keeps us focused and aware of these necessary truths!

MY NAME IS LOVE

Want to know where you are in your walk with God… Look at how you see Him in your prayers!

GOD… Is Re-

Renew our commitment Lord. Refocus us to see and to walk in our purpose for this union. Replenish our hearts with room for each other. Revive our desire to love. Realign our motives to do good for each other; to be good to each other.

Readjust our thinking; our sight, to see each other correctly and through Your eyes Lord. Reinvent our passion towards each other. Replace foolishness with peace. Reset our garden of trust and never let us abuse it again. Resuscitate; breathe life into our union. Restore the joy. Repair the damage we've caused. Regenerate our union to a higher place than it ever was before.

God, You are Re… Please do again what we can't. Reach where our arms can't go. Touch what our hands can't fix. Restore what we've taken for granted. Revive what we can not make alive again. Bring life to the death and damage we've caused in our foolishness, in our selfishness, in our inability to see and appreciate. Forgive us Lord, for going astray in our minds, in our memories and thoughts.

Renew our sight to see, not as what was, but as what will be; and what You have already ordained for us. Give us fertile ground to receive an abundance of love within our hearts. Recreate and restore the images we once had for each other that drew us together. Resuscitate life into our union. Repair it with the glue of trust, devotion, commitment and communication. Draw us back into the light. Rescue us from the darkness. Re-center, realign us with Your will, Your plans and Your purpose for joining us together. May our hearts never look back in anger, disgust or regret. Heal us from all of these things, and let the baggage of them remain in our past; never to be revisited.

Regenerate our thoughts, our desires, our motives and intents towards one another to remain in the light always. Remind us how far You've brought us, taken us and blessed us.

You've fixed us; repaired us when we were stuck. When we couldn't see our way. When we couldn't see past each other. When we couldn't see to appreciate each other. The separation didn't destroy us, it gave us a chance. A chance to heal. The opportunity to mend our wounds, and not make them worse or larger. You gave us a chance to refocus. To see anew what we first saw in each other. God, You do nothing for destruction… You repair!

The enemy thought he was ruining the purpose of God in our marriage. He was actually building a platform, for us to glorify God. He thought he was tearing down. He was actually building a bridge, providing us free passage back home to each other's hearts, where we will never leave again. He thought he had broken. He actually served as the glue which repaired us so we'll never leak again.

When something is broken, when we are broken… God is Re… Restorer, Repairer, Renewer, Rejuvenator, Reviver, Re-constructor, Replenisher, Replacer; Repositioner!

God is Re!

Chapter 4

AS RELATED TO GOD

~ God is Not an… In the way we expect it type of God. Accept it! Get use to it! ~

GOD REQUIRED

Doing what God requires of us doesn't enslave us… It makes us free!

I never understood this principle until now. God doesn't assign things to us to restrict us. He's not a taskmaster. He assigns a purpose to each one of our lives and gives us the privilege to walk in it.

The problem is… We don't see life that way. We see life through the lenses that we originated from our mothers and fathers, and our life is our own. We decide what to do with our lives, what we'll be, who we'll marry and so on. Our lives are about us, and what we decide to make of them. We answer only to ourselves for the direction we're headed. We're our own ship's captain.

Everything about that was a lie! We did not originate from our mothers and fathers. We were created through them by the grace and wisdom of God. We did not cross the bounds of space and time through birth and arrive empty handed either. What came with us on our first day of life, was our purpose. Seldom seen, unrecognizable at birth, it would

AS RELATED TO GOD

be the reason for our allowance in life and on Earth. It's what we least consider; yet is the most important part of us!

We don't live life all willy nilly! We're here on assignment from God. First to please Him and honor Him. Secondly, to walk out His will for our lives on Earth; called Purpose!

Our minds, hearts and thoughts must be retracted. We must be brought back to the truth of our existence. We will never live life fulfilled walking outside of the assignments of our lives.

But you say… I'm a successful businessman and a multimillionaire. I can buy anything I want in life. I have the best of everything! God would say to you… Son, unless you are using all that you spoke about, by the way; that I gave you, in life for your purpose which is attached to helping others… You really have nothing. Each day you have all material things; yet are empty inside.

The wisest and richest man of his time; Solomon had these things. But he used one word more than any in his life and writings… VANITY! He cried out; I have everything a man could want, but it's leaves me empty inside!

Only God and purpose fills the void of emptiness in our lives. We've been off track for so long. No one ever told us these things. It's why our lives are unfulfilled no matter how much success or wealth we obtain.

God designed our lives to respond to the purpose within us. It's called fulfillment. It's an awakening in our lives. This is what places us our our right and proper paths.

Let me explain this… You may be the top athlete in the world making millions of dollars, but if you are using those abilities to just help

MY NAME IS LOVE

yourself and a few around you; then you're walking in your gift… Not your purpose!

Our purpose is Always tied and connected to others. Our purpose is not what we do for ourselves… It's what we do for others! We'll be burdened; moved inside towards a particular cause, people or hardship. This becomes our niche in life. This is what we do besides go to our jobs. Our jobs help us make a living… Finding, knowing, and walking in our purpose… Makes Us Alive!

The purpose of God within and upon our lives doesn't restrict us… It makes us free. I've never lived such an amazing life until I began walking in my purpose. It didn't close the world around me; it opens it up immensely!

Many of the writings God gives to me are about marriage. It's of great concern to God because it's tied to our families and society. We've been lead so far away from the truth in marriage today. Instead of marriages being in order; they're in chaos and confusion. We subject our children to our foolishness and poor decisions too. It's not fair to them! We must stop; for our sakes and for theirs!

Order and submission is required of both husband and wife in marriage. Let's get that straight right out of the gate! The Bible says… "Husbands, love your wives, just as Christ loved the church and gave himself up for her!" Ephesians 5:25 Or is willing to lay down his life for her and die for her if necessary. Christ; a sinless man, laid down His life for sinners. It was the ultimate act of love.

The Bible also says this… "Wives, submit to your husbands as unto the Lord. For the husband is the head of the wife as Christ is the head of the church, his body, of which he is the Savior. In this same way, husbands ought to love their wives as their own bodies. He who loves his wife loves himself." Ephesians 5:22-33

AS RELATED TO GOD

For too long; especially women, have seen this as a punishment from God; not a proclamation of freedom! Why! Because we've been lied to, misinformed; and ignorant to the truth.

The proclamations and commandments of God are not there to restrict us; but to give us liberty within boundaries. Life without boundaries is chaos and confusion.

To prove my revelation from God, I recently asked a dear friend of mine a question. In the past, she told me when she was married she asked a question of God. "God, how can I submit to a man like this!"

What she learned from God will help every woman today in marriage. God showed her that all that He required of her was to do her part. If the husband didn't do his part, she was to go to God; not complain and nag her husband. "I let God deal with him; she said."

I asked her, how did it make you feel when you submitted yourself unto God in her marriage. These are the words she spoke… "IT MADE ME FREE!"

Submission doesn't enslave a woman… It sets her free! She no longer struggled with the curse of disobedience from Adam. She rose above it and it no longer bound her. She found her place and purpose and walked in it in Peace and freedom. "God freed me in every area of my life because I was submitting to God, through my husband!" Those were the beautiful words she spoke to me. I'll never forget them.

Men and women both, God is calling us all to peace and freedom in our lives by waking in the purpose assigned to each one of our lives individually and collectively through our marriages. Obedience is not the restriction of God… It's where we find liberty through purpose!

NO ONE EVER TOLD US

No one ever tells us this… But the Bible tells us that submission is required of Both Husband and Wife! Without submission from both, we have chaos… Which is the opposite of God's order. Or in simpler terms… Rebellion!

The reason why the Bible specifically tells wives to submit to their husbands, goes back to the disobedience of Adam and Eve. Part of the punishment for their disobedience was disruption in their relationship. Where there was once only peace, harmony and no thought of one over another; now there would be conflict. Now the eyes of their understanding would be enlightened to both good and evil. Before; they had known only good. In the good environment, conflict didn't exist. The desire to take over didn't exist. Rebellion didn't exist. Now, a woman would hate this word submission; unwisely, for a few reasons.

The first and most popular reason for her hatred would be because of the misuse and misinterpretation of the word. Secondly, she would hate it because of Adam. Because of Adam's sin, order would now be dictated by God in marriage. And God would hold the man responsible for the wife and his family. Before the fall, they only had one commandment from God… "Do not eat of the forbidden fruit." Genesis 2:17 Sin multiplied the commandments of God from One for Adam, and Ten to us and Moses.

Sin multiplies and causes the need for the Creator to place parameters around His creation. If we won't govern ourselves; God will govern us with rules and restrictions for our own safety and benefit.

The main ingredient; the substance of submission is Strength. Just as in faith; it's essence is Hope. If there's no strength; then it's another word entirely. Submission has everything to do with strength, power and abilities.

AS RELATED TO GOD

The one we look to for our ultimate definition of submission is Jesus... God in the flesh amongst humanity. Jesus had All strength, all power; all abilities, but maneuvered them to fall in alignment with the will of God assigned to His life and purpose.

As Christians, this now becomes our new, accurate and truthful definition of submission... The maneuverability of our strengths, powers and abilities to fall in alignment for our lives and purpose through marriage!

Did Jesus still contain all the strength of God in His human state? Yes, of course He did! But He maneuvered that strength, power and ability to fall in alignment with what God wanted Him to do with it. That's called Submission... Having great strength, power and abilities, yet maneuvering these strengths and using them within the purpose of God.

So let the truth be told today... Women are not weak, powerless and lack abilities. God Himself gave her those qualities. But He didn't give her these qualities to take over the very reason she was created. God is a god of order. Order is His first unwritten commandment for all He created. Look at the sun, moon; gravity. It all obeys the order ordained by God.

A WOMAN'S GREATEST DESIRE

It's a woman's greatest desire to be these things... If only she would yield to them!

She would find her life completely turned around. She would find she no longer has to fuss or holler to get what she wants. She would find she would not have to try to manipulate or control. She would have the things she desires with ease.

MY NAME IS LOVE

What would allow a woman to receive these things she isn't receiving now from her husband? How could she make just one adjustment in her life and have these things and more? The simple answer is… It's her Choice! All she must do is decide to make this change with one simple element of her life, and her husband will do all she ask within reason.

The change she must make lies within her Voice and her Words! A woman is a Multiplier! If she builds her husband up, he'll build her a castle. If she tears him down, he'll build her a shack.

She determines the home or the shack simply by the choice of her voice and her words.

A woman must first find a man she believes in. Not just someone she's attracted to, but someone she can believe in who he is, and where he's going in life. This is called potential. A woman can either multiply a man's potential or divide it.

Beyond the love, there is life. There's work, jobs, employment; careers. There's making a living to survive and thrive in life. There's so much more to love than attraction and the physical benefits. There's love where the two work together to form a family and a household.

To do this, they must believe in each other before they cross over into marriage. A woman must know a man's dreams, his goals; where he's headed way before she says… 'I do!' This is who she's really marrying beyond the looks. It the real man; how he lives, how he survives in life.

A woman can't be blind nor distracted to these things. It's the main reason she'll lose respect for him later. It falls within one of her basic needs of security; which falls under a man providing a safe environment for her, protecting her and providing for her. A woman must find these basic necessities in a man before marriage; or it won't last.

AS RELATED TO GOD

Once she's found the right man she can believe in, who can provide her with the security she needs; It's up to her to use the tools given to her by God.

Ladies this is the secret to a man doing what you need of him and more. It's not really a secret, because God gave us the answer in Proverbs Chapter 31 in the Bible. It says… "Who can find a virtuous woman. For her price is far above rubies. The heart of her husband doth safely trust in her, so that he shall have no need of spoil. She will do him good and not evil all the days of her life. Her husband is known in the gates, when he sits among the elders of the land. Her children arise up, and call her blessed; her husband also, and he praises her."

Simply with the choice of her words and attitude towards her husband, he's prosperous on his job; in his career, in the community and the way he's perceived by others. He praises her as do her children. She's a woman worthy of praise as she has understood the principles of God given to her in marriage. She understands that it was God who created the woman for the man He created. She understands her role and walks in it.

She knows she pleases God in this; as her husband can walk in his purpose for the family given to him by God. She helps him discover who he is. Her encouragement and kindness motivated him to want to succeed and excel in life. She made him feel proud about himself, so he took his place in society with confidence. He came home and praised and admired her for allowing him to be the fullness of who God created him to be.

It's a beautiful thing to see, a marriage in harmony; not in competition. How that pleases God, for a marriage to align according to how He intended it to.

MY NAME IS LOVE

The woman holds the keys to the status of the household. If she speaks kindly to her husband; of him, and lifts him up... There's nothing he won't do for her. He'll bend over backwards and do flips for her. It's the power of her words and attitude towards him.

But if she tears him down; talks down to him and about him... She'll get what that brings also; a defeated man with little or no direction in his life.

Proverbs also gives us this overlooked secret to to a woman's success in marriage. Proverbs 30:31 also gives us this overlooked secret to a woman's success in marriage. It says... "Favor is deceitful, and beauty is vain: but a woman that fears the Lord, she shall be praised." Proverbs 31:30 The fear of the Lord is not to be afraid of Him, but to reverence and praise Him. This is ultimately why the woman made the choice to honor her husband through her words and attitude... She did it in reverence to God and His commands for an excellent marriage.

A woman's greatest desire is to be who God created her to be. If her desire is for marriage, she fulfills that desire by being the woman God intended her to be for her husband. In this she honors God. In this the Bible says... "Give her of the fruit of her hands; and let her own works praise her in the gates." Proverbs 31:31

She has followed the commandment of God through marriage. She's become a virtuous woman... Worthy of praise!

SEE THE TRUTH...

In the beginning when things are fresh and new...

You slip a little in feelings, you gain a little. You fall short in respect, in some ways you gain respect. It's the cycles of a relationship.

AS RELATED TO GOD

If you won't do it now when things are all shiny and new, you won't do it when things are old and rusty.

Set the precedence and continue it. Otherwise you're just deceiving someone. The other side of marriage shouldn't change; it shouldn't digress… but grow. Marriage fails when one or both neglect to fulfill the bargain they agreed to while dating. You loved who they were and what you saw, or you would have moved on before going into the permanent relationship of marriage. But each of you moved forward based on the parameters of feelings, love and respect. You moved forward believing this was the person you would receive and more. It's who and what you were shown. It's what you expected and based your decision of forever on.

Marriage is not a place for a woman to let her hair down and a man to kick off his shoes. It's not the place of let down! 'Oh, now that I'm married, I let down my standards!' No!

Your let down is a breach of your promise. Your let down is not what caused that person to sacrifice all others on Earth for you to pretend to be someone you weren't. Your let down is a bill of goods your spouse didn't purchase. You were contracted for who and what they saw in the dating and engagement realm and greater.

Men believe… 'Oh now that I'm married, I can kick my shoes off and it doesn't matter if my feet smell like corn chips, or I now pass gas in front of this precious woman God has given me. Now I can really be myself!' You lied! No way that woman would have put up with your carelessness while dating.

We put on our best attitudes, manners and outfits while charming a woman. You're lying to her if you're someone other than the facade you're presenting. A facade is like a fake building. It looks real and beautiful on the outside, but on the inside; it's empty!

MY NAME IS LOVE

Women believe… 'Oh I got him now, I can let my hair down.' The beauty she displayed while dating, she now puts less effort into. The romance that was booming before marriage, now just fizzles. Now, that sweet and gentle voice has become hard and unrecognizable. Where it use to comfort and edify, it now finds fault and criticizes. Now instead of building a haven for her husband, she's now built a wall for him to shelter and hide himself from the barbs. He shuts down because he's torn down. Something God never intended him to be in his home and family. Where he once sought to communicate, he now avoids it… Sheltering himself from the storm.

One or both have lied, or broken their promises of who and what they were. Sure things change when two people come together with different lives and backgrounds to form one unit of a family, but the agreement was set before the marriage on who you were, and who you were going to be. Dating was just a preview of what you were purchasing with love and commitment.

Let down or lies have entered in. Forever has become for only now. Blame has entered in, instead of responsibility. Lies and laziness has entered, instead of commitment.

Marriage is not the place for games, immaturity, and for those who can't uphold their promises and commitments. Marriage is not the place for losing your identity, but gaining it. It's not the place for the selfish and self centered. It's an agreement to die to self for the benefit of the other. It's not the place to spread your wings, but to clip them, and to build your nest of love and togetherness.

If you can't be this and greater in your dating… Please don't ruin someone else's life by crossing over into marriage!

AS RELATED TO GOD

WHAT IF WE COULD FIND OUR PURPOSE IN LOVE

What if we could find our purpose in love. What if we chose love, not just for looks, but for purpose. What if it was the place we fit. What if it was our assignment as a man to lead, and as a woman; to assist the purpose assigned to the family by God.

What if we chose purpose over being fine, beautiful; having a great body, muscles or some of the shallow things in life absent of substance.

What if we were holding it down for God and for His Kingdom. What if we took our proper place in our marriages, homes and families and brought forth bright and productive members of society. What if we blocked out everything the world thought was hip, cool and fashionable. What if we provided a stable, loving, healthy environment for our families to grow, prosper and to one day establish great families of their own.

What if that was walking in your purpose. What if being a good husband was your purpose; leading your family, loving your wife and children. Being a model, an example; a productive citizen. People noticing you, and your lifestyle, without you standing on a street corner preaching with a bull horn.

What if your purpose was being a wife of modest and kind words who loved, and respected your husband as unto the Lord. What if you blocked out all of the noise of your single girlfriends, family and decided 'I'm gonna hold this thing down for God and for the building of His Kingdom.'

What if you both husband and wife, died to self and pride; and loved each other without line or limit. What if pride was gone, and all that came out of your mouth was beautiful words of love and kindness. What if you praised and built up each other; and your children, your

MY NAME IS LOVE

neighbors, your co-workers and even perfect strangers noticed the pure, respectful love that you exhibited towards each other. What if others wanted it, and were drawn to it as a light; and thirsted for it as salt.

What if you found your purpose by loving, and supporting your husband. As the woman in Proverbs 31, who sold herself out by unselfishly holding it down for her husband, her children and for God. She was the envy of all who entered her presence.

She wasn't weak by any means. Laying down your life for a bigger purpose is the definition of Strength. Doing what everyone else is doing requires no restraint at all. But making up your mind to hold it down in your marriage, home and family, is an exhibition of true strength, integrity and character.

Not all of us seek these things, but we that follow Christ; they should top our agendas. The problem is, we as Christians can live too close to the world. We mimic, instead of being original. We follow, instead of leading. We worry about appearing weak to our friends, by being committed to our spouses and to God's plan over our lives.

Misery loves company! They want us where they are; unhappy and jumping from one bad relationship to another. Instead, they should be coming to us for advice on how we allowed God to bring us a good partner and a healthy and productive relationship.

THE WOMAN DIDN'T UPSET THE BALANCE OF THE WORLD WHEN SHE ATE

Ladies, the world didn't fall when Eve ate of the forbidden fruit in the garden. It fell into chaos only when Adam ate. Why? Because God gave the commandment to the man. When they hid themselves after they sinned, God came looking for the man; not the woman. It was he whom God placed overall responsibility within.

The woman was created to assist the man in the plans and purpose of God. The Bible tells us in Genesis 3:9... "But the LORD God called to the man and said to him, Where are you?" How can that which is created; be over that which it was created for! It can't, and it should never be. When a woman leads over her husband, she is out of her place, and out of the order God ordained for marriage.

Why is God telling us this? Because for too long our marriages and families have been out of alignment. We have allowed the world to tell us what was right and in order... Rather than God!

The woman has raised herself up over the man. She has despised her role; rather than embrace it. Because when she walked in it, the world told her she was weak for her obedience to God and her husband. The same with the man. The world has told him he was weak for dedicating himself to one woman and his family; when it was more fun having many women and no commitments and obligations. Again, this is what the world has dictated to us, and even we as Christians have fallen for it. It should never be, that the world tells us how to live. Definitely not how to run our marriages.

Marriage is not the property of the world. It falls under the jurisdiction of God; His rules, His requirements and His obligations. The problem is... We've never been told this!

Women hate the word submission. But she fails to see that God requires submission of the man first. We've been taught wrongly about this word. It's absolute strength; not weakness! There's nothing weak at all about submission. Its true definition is... Laying your strength aside for a purpose greater than your own. Jesus had all the power in the world. He was God in the flesh. There was nothing He couldn't do. Yet, He governed His strength to walk in alignment with the plans and purpose of God; His father, for His life on Earth.

In marriage, the man must love his wife as Christ loved the church, and must lay down his life for her as needed; and as necessary. This is what a man following God attempts to do.

The world has skewed even our Christian definitions, and instead of seeing this as the right man God has for her to prosper with; a woman see's him as a man she can control!

YOU INSPIRE ME TO GREATNESS

With you I'm on my path to greatness. She found her purpose helping me walk in mine!

It's not that you can't be this for a man. It's that you must find a man you can be this for and allow yourself to be it!

A woman will find her purpose through the man/family. She will find what's been lacking and limited in her life. She will find exuberance when she comes in alignment and discovers the reason for her living called purpose.

This is where she's supposed to be. This is who she is. This is where creativity meets with existence. This is where she finds her house and makes it home. This is where she multiplies and increases. This is where she expands and enlarges everything around her.

She has found her place in life. She has accepted it with her entirety. She has become a life changer. Whatever she touches, she multiplies. She was created to assist; to come along side of and increase. Not herself; but the connectivity of her purpose. She's a life changer; a path illuminator. She gives what is absent and lacking. She fills in gaps and

AS RELATED TO GOD

crevices never known or imagined. We are less than without her. She lies unfulfilled without the attachment of us.

Oh, if we all could see the beauty of God assigned to our lives and purpose; we would run to them rather than rebel from them.

A change is coming, where we must split from the world; the ways of the world. Jesus will return for His bride, without spot or wrinkle. This no way resembles our lives, marriages and families today. So there must be a change; an awakening to return home to the principles and commandments of God.

There must be a realigning for the preparation; for the return of Christ. We must depart from our foolish, selfish and worldly ways that have become a part of our lives so subtly, that we have not recognized that we stand alongside the ways of the world; not examples to them.

The change must start in our marriages, our homes, our families… But first in our hearts! We must make up our minds and decide that we'll no longer allow the world to dictate our lives, marriages and decisions.

There are two words which separates us from the world; rebellious and obedient. In rebellion we walk along side the world. We mimic their behaviors, actions and attitudes. In obedience, we align our lives with the word of God; separate and distinct from what the world is doing.

Families are the rudder that steers our society. Ladies, you are the Key to Life! God has deemed you number one essential to His purpose. This is not to cause you to boast; nor to fill you full of pride. It's to humble you in humility, and to repent for not taking your rightful places in your marriages and homes. The elevation of God should never fill us with pride; but bring us to our knees seeking forgiveness.

MY NAME IS LOVE

All along ladies, you have been the key to the success or failure of our homes. No, you have not always had good and decent men to lead you correctly; love and cherish you as God intended. But those of you that have, and will have such a man; must know this truth from God... As good and as obedient as a man is, he can never lead unless you Allow him to!

We have allowed the world to misalign our definition of leadership with... 'I ain't lettin no man tell me what to do!' Just then, you have stepped out of your purpose for your creation from God, and disqualified yourself to be married.

We have confused marriage as playing house like when we were children. We have confused it for the wedding, the wedding dress, the ring and the honeymoon. The true definition of marriage is a union of three; not two. That third person is God. He's the most important person; that we leave out. We must understand that marriage is not a man nor a woman institution... It's a God institution! And when we institute with God, we must come in alignment with His rules for the institution.

There's no changing the rules. No making your own vows to suit your selfish plan and agenda, so you can wander around doing what you want. You've entered God's territory when you took on marriage! You must go by His rules; not yours!

If you can't be a man to lead, and a woman to allow him to lead; then marriage isn't for you! We've been fooled too long into believing that marriage is the place we land to fulfill our sexual needs and selfish agendas. It's not; and it can no longer be!

Marriage is not yours... It's God's. Take your hands off of it. It's not yours to change! We enter it with excitement; when we should enter it with Fear & Trembling!

The world doesn't dictate who we are. Yet we've allowed it to tell us, and we've paid an awful price. Our families and homes are in chaos, disarray and confusion! We can only be light to the world when we move away from it, and take our proper place in obedience to God and purpose.

This is a chastening of our hearts from God of what He expects of us. We all must fall in alignment to this truth.

PURPOSE OF MARRIAGE

The Purpose of God assigned over the family… It's the one thing we're unaware of and one of the most important reasons for our marriage. The one thing that ruins more marriages… Is the belief that it's the place to get our needs met… And that's all! We've never thought of the needs and examples we're required to meet for others through our marriage. The truth is, purpose is never about us. Purpose is, and will always be about meeting a need, or being an example to a smaller or larger entity than ourselves. No one ever told us… The Purpose of God resides over, and is attached to our marriages once we enter them. One of those attached purposes is to be Light & Salt to the marriages of the world. One of those purposes is to model marriage in love and Christ to our children; so marriages are blessed in their generations.

How will they know how to honor an institution created and ordained by God, if they're not shown by us as Christians. The trouble is, our marriages are poor and inadequate examples to them. So they don't look to us as models; they look deeper within themselves and to the world for their examples. They move further away from the precepts of God.

This isn't to say that you have to be a Christian to be married. But I would say this… It can be hard enough with both members confessing they're Christian's. I wouldn't want to imagine being yoked with someone who is unaware or disregards the commandments of God.

MY NAME IS LOVE

One who has no fear or reverence for His precepts. I wouldn't want to live and be bound by one who lacks discipline, respect, and is unaware of the fear of the Lord. It can be difficult enough with those claiming they're Christian's, yet baring no fruit of it. I wouldn't even want to imagine being bound to less.

I SHALL DECLARE A THING, AND IT SHALL COME TO PASS

God declares a thing and it is! It is at that very moment of declaration… Done! Time, timing and purpose; catch up to His declarations and manifest them into the tangible atmosphere of our lives.

Nothing returns to Him unaccomplished, unfinished; undone! Nothing! Once it leaves His mind or His mouth; whatever it is; is done! Not once, has any word God sent or spoken returned to Him empty; void of its contents and accomplishment. Nothing has ever returned to Him with reason or excuse… Only Completion!

His word is Absolute! If He spoke it… It will yield it's harvest!

Chapter 5

THE SIN DEBT OF ADAM

~We'll never solve spiritual equations… With earthly logic! ~

THE SIN DEBT OF ADAM

The insight given by God in this chapter can Save Countless Marriages and Families!

AND SO IT BEGAN…

The great fight! The great Destroyer of marriage & family! It would be responsible for the ruin of more marriages than anything. It would destroy more families than anything. The saddest part of all… We had no clue of what it was that destroyed us. So we put the blame on each other… And out of ignorance; the fight continued amongst ourselves, producing havoc and ruin in our lives!

It's gone on for countless generations unknown; hidden away from our awareness. Only those who have walked in obedience to God in submission, have been able to maneuver around such destruction. The rest of us have wandered aimlessly; not having a clue what was driving us to beat the air.

MY NAME IS LOVE

The greatest enemy is the one that remains hidden, and causes us to look at others as our problems... Rather than seeing the issue lies within us; not our spouse.

Because of this sin debt in marriage; we face each other face to face, rather than side by side. Look how far a couple can walk facing each other! Not far at all, until they quickly run out of space. But place the couple side by side; arm in arm, and the journey becomes endless.

A face to face relationship is confrontational; competitive. It leads us nowhere. A side by side relationship is one born in partnership, togetherness; teamwork. The couple moved forward without all the nonsense of arguing, fighting; barb throwing. In this relationship, you want the best for each other. You inspire each other and lift each other up.

We never knew such things until now. So we blamed each other for our mess. We kept blaming each other for our messes until we ruined our marriages. While the enemy sat back and laughed at us. 'Another marriage destroyed and all I had to do was turn them on themselves'... He sits back and says! Too easy!

Neither seen or heard; he simply turned the couple to face each other; rather than to walk side by side as they were ordained.

Another marriage ruined; another family in disarray!

GOD PROVIDES WISDOM FOR US TO AVOID THIS...

Adam and his wife lived in complete peace and harmony. They were the only two humans to ever have intimate and face to face fellowship with God. Nothing was hidden nor withheld from them.

THE SIN DEBT OF ADAM

They lived in a perfect world. There was no conflict or confusion. There was no leading, and no one being led. There was only responsibility that God gave to His first created; man. God is a god of order, and man would answer to Him for his deeds on Earth, and for his family.

There was no man versus woman struggle. Pride had not entered the world. There was only peace and harmony amongst them until… The price of their disobedience threw the world and the harmonic dynamic between man and God out of balance. Pride, confusion, an attempt to control, and chaos had now entered life, the world; and the relationship between man and woman!

The Bible tells us this… "And you will desire to control your husband, but he will rule over you." Genesis 3:16

This sin put the woman at war with her husband! This is the One Scripture that man and woman must Know, Recognize and take to heart Before they Enter into Marriage. If not, it will be there waiting to ruin their marriage!

Husband and wife must first agree to die to self and pride before they enter marriage, or this curse will cripple their relationship. The husband must agree to take his place as the head, as a role of overall responsible for his family. The wife must agree to take her role as a help, and supportive role for God's purpose for the family. Neither of their roles are to each other; but unto God.

We must stop all this nonsense that's in today's marriages. God requires order in our marriages; not chaos. This describes the modern marriage of today; even the Christian ones.

Man is not the boss, but the leader. He doesn't dictate orders. He leads by example. He doesn't first seek to get his needs met. He seeks to first meet the needs of his wife and children. His is not an authoritative

MY NAME IS LOVE

role, but a responsible role. He seeks not to rule over his wife, but to lead her in the love of Christ.

Women receive their roles from God. She was taken from the side of man to be by his side. She wasn't meant to lead, to control through manipulation; but to help and support the purpose of the family given by God. A woman at the head of a family is like a cow at the circus with two heads… It's a freak!

Both must lead in their respective roles. The virtuous woman in Proverbs 31, allowed her husband to take his role as she took hers. Because she did, he took his place amongst the elders. He was respected in the community and in his career. Because she allowed him to be who God created him to be, he praised her. Because she was an example of a loving wife and mother; her children praised her. Because she walked in her gifts given to her by God, and she used her mind and words through wisdom and kindness; all of the people she traded with respected and honored her.

When a woman learns these truths, she can have an incredible marriage, because there's nothing her husband won't do to please her when she walks in her role from God. My friend once shared with me an example of this truth.

A woman's words hold tremendous weight. The Bible tells us… "Death and Life are in the power of the tongue." Proverbs 18:21 A woman's words can build a man up or tear him down. She can speak into existence a Prince or a Pauper. It's up to her, through the kindness or destructiveness of her words!

Here's the example of my friend. She and her husband would go to the grocery store, and when they got home he asked her to help with the bags. She didn't like carrying the bags! One day instead of carrying grocery bags, my friend used her wisdom instead. These are the simple

THE SIN DEBT OF ADAM

words she spoke to her husband… "Wow, look at my strapping man carrying all of those bags!" She never carried another grocery bag!

She properly used what God gave her as a woman. She used softness and praise, and it moved her husband never to ask her to help with the bags again.

It's what every man longs to hear from his wife… Praise & Respect! There's nothing he won't do for you if you learn these simple truths. But why don't women do this if it's works so well and it's so easy! Sometimes they've chosen the wrong man that refuses to take his place. Sometimes they have the right man and they just refuse to do it because of pride. The Bible tells us… "Pride goes before destruction and a haughty spirit before a fall." Proverbs 16:18 There's our answer there.

A woman must make up her mind before she enters marriage that she can be these things; not after she's married. So many marriages are ruined because she appears to be these things during the engagement period, and once they're married… She changes! Instead of cooperation, she seeks to control. Instead of all of those kind words she once spoke; she now criticizes, puts him down and disrespects him. Some of it's the fault of the man, who didn't hold up his end of the bargain. Some of it's the woman's fault. Regardless of fault, it must be fixed with putting aside our pride and foolishness.

It's the repercussions from the disobedience of Adam; not his wife, but Adam. The command of God was given to the man. Adam still could have lived forever after his wife ate of the forbidden fruit. The woman would have died, but he would still be alive today.

This one thing has caused more divorces, ruined more marriages, homes and families than anything. Out of ignorance, or just flat out pride; we fall for the enemies tricks daily. We not only affect our lives, but the lives and futures of our children also. IT MUST STOP!

MY NAME IS LOVE

We as husbands and wives, must learn to navigate around this marriage killer. This was set in place thousands of years before us, but it's still prevalent today. We can no longer afford to ignore this punishment from Adam's sin, because it applies to everyone of us in marriage even today.

So how do we kill the marriage killer! Men, we kill it with love, care and sacrifice for our wives. Wives, you kill it with soft words, kindness and respect towards your husband. All pride has to go! The woman in Proverbs 31 knew this secret and cast all of her pride aside.

Soft doesn't equate to weakness; especially with God! On the contrary, it takes strength to be obedient to God's commands, precepts and principals. The soft and gentle words a woman speaks to her husband is as strength spoken from the mouth of God. A man would move mountains for a woman who praises him. It's the greatest strength a woman has… Her words, kindness and encouragement.

For too long we've been tricked, fooled and lead astray into believing the lies of the world. The world's standard for being a strong woman is being loud, boisterous and condemning towards her man. Pride and her single girlfriends tells her that being a virtuous woman is weak. She falls for the lies, and she seeks to control rather than falling in line with the principals of God and marriage. 'I won't let him tell me what to do,' she says. 'So I'll confuse him by withholding affection, and making him feel less than.' She disrespects him, his role, and his position in the marriage and the household. She got what she wanted. She's taken control of the family. She's brought with her, chaos and confusion; as she's stepped outside of her role, and of the will of God.

Too many marriages and homes resemble this example. Our marriages are out of alignment. Not only are our children and families suffering as a result of this… Society is!

THE SIN DEBT OF ADAM

Man must take his God given place in our marriages and homes, and the woman must allow him to! She must be wise to recognize that Adam's sin put her at war against her husband; if she follows her flesh. There are two ways she can avoid this. One is to love God more than her husband. By doing so, her commitment and accountability is to God. Her husband will receive the residual affects from her first love to God. Secondly, she must be disciplined and wise to know, this is a pitfall to ruin her marriage. She can remedy this with her gifts from God. Her gifts from God include her femininity, soft spoken and kind words, and praise and encouragement towards her husband.

No one has ever told us these things, and it's the reason our marriages have failed. If we never know the source of the problem, we can never fix the problem!

The solution has come to us all this day. Adam's sin came with a marriage killer amongst other hardships. A woman will bring forth children in pain during childbirth, is one of those repercussions. "A woman will desire to rule over her husband, but he shall rule over her is another." Genesis 3:16

The pain in childbirth can not be changed. But the marriage killer can and must be! Know this truth before you enter marriage. Be prepared with the wisdom God provides; and be blessed.

Your children and their marriages will be blessed also because you've learned, obeyed and walked within this truth.

TRICKED, FOOLED & DECEIVED

How could two people so in love; now can't stand one another! How can two, so inseparable, end up divorced!

MY NAME IS LOVE

Something happened! You don't marry to get divorced. Nothing could separate the two of you before. You were so in love. You planned on forever. Forever didn't come!

Unless you went into the marriage lying about your true intentions; unless you weren't the person you said you were before you entered marriage... You've been tricked, fooled and deceived out of your marriage. You've been robbed of your forever. Your peace has been exchanged for loneliness, or foolishness from wrong people... People that have no intentions of marriage, commitment or forever. They want only what they can distract from you now!

You were once one of One. Now you've become one of many. We've traded treasure for trinket. Treasures are kept. Trinkets are toyed with, then tossed aside; when they quickly lose their values in the one that holds them loosely.

It's not just our loss; but look at what we do to our children for our poor decisions. If two people that proclaim they belong to Christ can't stay married... Something's wrong! When we meet the pre exam requirements of being equally yoked to enter marriage, and we still can't stay married... Something's really wrong!

This is the truth that we've failed to see and it has ruined our marriages. God established marriage; not man. Marriage is God's institution; lent to man for the establishment of his family. We must know this... Whatever God loves; the enemy hates!

Family makes up society. What better way to ruin society than to ruin where it starts... The family through marriage! The enemy doesn't care if you get married. He wants to destroy it after you're married. That way he destroys more than one life, and causes a hole in society. Sometimes the damage can go on for generations; through the children and their marriages.

THE SIN DEBT OF ADAM

This must end! Enough is enough! We must open up our eyes to see the real cause of this destruction. If we went into marriage with true and sincere motives; then we must look at the true source of our problems... The enemy at work in our marriages.

We with blinders on, have only looked in front of us for the problems in our marriage. The sum of our problems has not been that person we see everyday. We've never thought of, or looked with wisdom for the real culprit of deceit.

The enemy hates our families! We might as well know the truth. He hates when our marriages work and are successful. He hates it when we, husband and wife, stay strong together and raise our children correctly; and they grow up with good examples for their marriages. These are lives saved from destruction and foolishness. These are productive lives in society. This is why it's so important that we know these truth and take the blinders off.

This is the enemy's plan... Take the focus off of himself by using any one of us that's weak. He looks for any chinks in our armor to cause distractions, and to keep us from moving forward in our purpose from God.

First, turn the couple on themselves. Cause them to see faults, rather than strengths. Instead of contentment; cause them to complain and nit pick about meaningless things. Instead of using voices for love and edification; turn the volume up to criticize and tear down. Instead of humility, only see fault in the other person... Not in yourself! Constantly blame, which is meaningless and counterproductive; leaving the situation worse. Shut down the lifeline of communication with pride; never saying you're sorry.

All of these things happen everyday in marriages, and we simply go unaware of the true cause. We're blind; because we can only see each other, rather than a real enemy seeking to destroy us. When we turn the focus inward instead of outward; we lose!

We must refocus. We must join in togetherness as one; united against the world for our marriage, our children and our homes. We must agree to take the focus off of each other; and see with wisdom, the traps and tricks of the enemy.

We must recognize these things quickly and not let them fester, and break down our communication. Isolate and conquer, has always been the plan of the enemy since Adam's time.

If you're weak, acknowledge it and talk about it. He'll attack the weakest one of us. It's why we're both different, and have strengths in different areas to assist each other.

Want to know when we're being tricked, deceived and fooled! Argue over nothing! Pick fights over petty, meaningless things. Complain about things, rather than being grateful for what you have and who you have. Tear down instead of edify. Control instead of love. Manipulate instead of cooperate. Listen to your friends; rather than the wisdom of God and others with sound advice.

Suffocate those feelings of ill content, and embrace your commitment to God and your spouse.

There's nothing more pleasing and pleasurable; than finding, and walking in our purpose from God, in life and marriage. It's where we truly fit; in life and the world. It brings with it great joy, peace and contentment. These things we'll never find in the world; absent of our purpose.

Know these truths. Recognize the enemy as the true culprit of destruction. Build your walls around your marriage with love, commitment, contentment and wisdom. If he's already caused destruction in your marriage... These truths from God are his eviction notice! Serve him his papers and be tricked, deceived and fooled; no more!

YOUR SENSES USE TO TELL YOU... NOW YOU MUST TELL YOUR SENSES

At first, in the beginning; our love is on automatic. Our hearts and minds are like lasers; focused on that person constantly. Our ideas flow with creativity and ingenuity to find ways to be together. We get the butterflies, the chills; the goose bumps, in their presence and absent from them. This is real! This is the one we've been praying for.

Everything is great! We marry. Now we see each other every day. The fascination subsides. We now question our decision. Did we choose correctly? This is when most marriages can go South. But they don't have to with wisdom and enlightenment.

Today, God showed me the secret to keeping our marriages on track... How they were for us in the beginning. This is what He showed me... At first our relationship is on Automatic. The feelings, the excitement; the jubilation all comes natural and easy... Automatic!

But this is what no one ever told us; and our marriages suffer, and can be ruined for the lack of knowledge of it. There will be a time in the beginning of our marriages when our feelings run on automatic; with little assistance from us. There will come a time when these automatic senses will transition to Manual senses.

These senses will be turned over to us to initiate!

This means that we; as both husband and wife, must govern these senses on our own. They become our responsibility! We are now the

MY NAME IS LOVE

ones responsible for producing those same feelings and more to keep our marriage new, exciting and moving forward.

So often we hear that same old excuse and cop out… 'We outgrew each other!' No, you were blind, and allowed your blindness to lead to the destruction of your marriage. There was nothing wrong with it.

No one ever told the both of you that in the beginning of your marriage, your heart, body and mind gave you a head start. It gave you a gigantic boost; which can normally last for many years. Your emotions and feelings ran on automatic. All marriages are different. But all will go through these two phases… Automatic and Manual senses.

Our marriages aren't something we discard like a piece of gum that's lost it's flavor. These are covenants with God. Covenants that require discipline and commitment.

When the sweetness leaves, our commitment remains! Let the truth be told… This is what we'll live and depend upon for the majority of our marriage… .Discipline & Commitment! It doesn't change. It was in those vows we made to God on our wedding day. We may have said them to each other, and before a crowd of witnesses, but those vows were made as a covenant to God. A covenant is a binding Contract with God!

When the boost wears off and we must take over the helms of our marriages; we must change. Where our hearts, bodies and minds once guided us in love, at some point; the responsibility will be shifted onto us.

When this happens, and it will! We'll now be prepared with the wisdom God has provided… Instead of our marriage perishing; like so many others without this understanding.

THE SIN DEBT OF ADAM

This is what we must do. We must manually tell ourselves everything our minds, bodies and hearts once told us automatically in the beginning without effort. This is when we initiate date nights, and other ways to keep the fire burning in our marriages.

I tell myself something. It becomes a belief. My belief becomes my reality! This is how it works. This is what we must do. We must constantly think and speak positively over our spouses and our marriages. We must confess these words as compliments, words of affirmation, thanks and gratitude to each other. Contrary to our beliefs... Our marriages don't run on their own. They need constant input and assistance from us. We were deceived in the beginning of our marriages by the boost of our emotions. This led us into a false belief that our marriages would always run on automatic. In each one, there'll be a transference in which we must step up and take the helm.

These things told us how beautiful, how handsome they were to us. They told us how blessed we were to have them. We must now use our own words to make these things realities in our minds and marriage. The Bible tells us... "As a man thinks in his heart, so is he." Proverbs 23:7

We must now tell ourselves these things and begin to see them as such in our minds. The ungrateful will see flaws instead of positive qualities. We must focus on the positive things we see. Recognize them, appreciate them, and speak them out; in love covered with tenderness and affection.

The Bible also says... "You shall also decree a thing, and it shall be established unto you." Job 22:28 This means we are either liberated or prisoners through our words! We must speak, and fill our own hearts with truth and positivity. We must tell ourselves as we once did... God gave me this person and I'm going to love them, care for them and cherish them always.

MY NAME IS LOVE

We must confess gratitude instead of criticism. We must confess to ourselves how thankful and grateful we are to have found someone we loved enough to marry, and share our lives with. We must remind ourselves how attracted we are to them; how desirable this person is to us. We must remember how things once were, and tell our minds these things. Our hearts and bodies will gravitate towards our confessions.

We must also see something that may have been lacking when we first married. We married for ourselves, for looks; for money or whatever reason. What we overlooked is God attached a purpose for our marriage once we entered. In other words, the marriage isn't all about you! It's much bigger than the couple involved. This should take our eyes off of our selfishness.

I once knew a woman that married a man. Many wondered why she stayed married to him. He was mean, and disrespectful. She continued to serve him; when so many women would have left him years ago.

One day, God gave me the answer why she never left him. These were the words God spoke to me… "Her marriage isn't about her!"

The light came on for me. Now I completely understood. This woman was like the woman in Proverbs Chapter 31. Although her husband prospered, praised her and called her blessed, he wasn't the reason she did the things she did for him.

This remarkable and amazing woman knew the secret to success in life! Not just in marriage. That secret was her respect and reverence for God. All she did was as unto the Lord. Her husband, her children and her community, were simply blessed from her obedience to God!

When the sparkles wear off in our marriage and we go from automatic senses to manual, we must adjust our thinking, our behavior and the words we speak to ourselves and to our spouses. We must tell ourselves that we love, appreciate, cherish and adore what God has given us. We must confess that appreciation through our words to keep the fires of our relationship burning bright. We must also know and confess, that God has assigned reason and purpose to our marriage; and we're determined to walk in it out of reverence and obedience to Him.

This is what a Christian marriage looks like. This is how the purpose of our marriage can be Light and Salt to others!

What once came easily and automatic for us, we must now know will one day cease. This has nothing to do with us; it's the natural progression of life and marriage. With this transition, we must use imagination, creativity and through prayer; the wisdom of God for the beautification of our lives through marriage.

Love is not a chore… It's a privilege! See it only that way!

HUMILITY… CAN WE FIND IT

"Blessed are the poor in spirit, for theirs is the Kingdom of Heaven." Matthew 5:3

The scripture didn't say poor in wallet; in bank account… But in spirit.

In others words Humility! Those who are humble in spirit, in their attitudes; in their behaviors and mannerisms towards life and others… Shall inherit and be entitled to the Kingdom of Heaven.

How do we get there? We humble ourselves! We forgo our pride. We place others before ourselves. We serve the needs of others.

Humility isn't walking around poor, dirty and insecure. Humility is an individual with substance! And they maneuver that substance towards the needs of others. Jesus did this! He wasn't poor. He contained all

MY NAME IS LOVE

wealth in Heaven & Earth. Yet, He laid it down for a period, and a purpose larger than Himself... You and I!

Many today are Christian in name; not in deed. They've given themselves the title, but don't contain the fruits.

The Bible says... "You will know them by their fruits. Do men gather grapes from thorn bushes or figs from thistles? Even so, every good tree bears good fruit, but a bad tree bears bad fruit. A good tree cannot bear bad fruit, nor can a bad tree bear good fruit. Every tree that does not bear good fruit is cut down and thrown into the fire. "Therefore by their fruits you will know them." Matthew 7:15-20

We don't and can't bear fruit living too close to the world. It's just not going to happen adopting their ways and mannerisms. It's not going to happen with pride either; nor an over exaggerated opinion of ourselves.

One thing many Christians fail to see is the gifts of God at work within us; humble us... Not puff us up! It's not us at work; it's God at work in and through our lives towards others.

The very meaning of a gift is something given to us by someone else. It's not something we produce ourselves. So how can we take credit for it, and walk in arrogance with it; if it didn't originate from us. We can't, and we shouldn't!

We as Christians first have to humble ourselves. We look no different than the world, bragging about who we are. God requires humility of all of us.

The world will never change seeing us as we are. They find nothing to drawn and motivate them towards Christ. They see us as no different than themselves. One can't be light to the other; unless and until, one stands as an example of what's right. Until one stands separate and distinct from the other. That other is us as Christians.

We must take our proper place in humility and service to a dying world. We must lay our pride and arrogance aside, and be Light and Salt as God ordained!

THANK YOU LORD…

Thank you Lord for opening our eyes to these truths as never seen before. To strengthen our marriages and families for success through wisdom… Instead of them failing; through the lack of knowledge and understanding!

THANK YOU FATHER!

Chapter 6

HELP US LORD

~ Mustard seed isn't mountain moving faith. A mustard seed that is the smallest of seeds, yet Grows into one of the largest plants is! ~

"Your writings are rendering me speechless. Keep your open heart and mind tuned into God's frequency and you will not go wrong. You will direct many."

Debra D'Attoma

MISUNDERSTOOD

Two of the things we misinterpret as Christian's are the Anointing of God and Holiness.

We do many things in church not truly understanding why. We even come up with our own beliefs about the things of God by not fully understanding His word. We do things out of tradition.

Holiness and the Anointing of God are some of these things. How do we display holiness at church?

Holiness is what we display outside of church, after church, during the week... Through our lifestyles! How do we demonstrate holiness for a few hours in a building on Sunday! Any of us can dress up our behavior for a few hours. What's important is who we are after, and outside of church. Therein lies the truth of who we really are, and how we align with holiness.

There's one of us that's holy at church; and His name is God. The rest of us can try to impress, perform, compete for who's the holiest during the service! Again, here we are carrying on traditions and misinterpretations of the Word of God. To grow and be placed on our proper paths, we must be released from untruths.

Do we even know what holiness looks like. It's not what most of us think. We use it on Sunday; no other day of the week, as our Spiritual Barometer. It's what we use to measure our spirituality against our neighbor's.

We think it makes us dance when they play that one song! The better our two-step, the more holy we are! No! That just means we have rhythm and can dance!

We believe the anointing is making a lot of noise, or running around the pews. We have conjured in our own minds something we've adopted as godly and displayed it. We have missed the mark!

Let's talk about King Saul. He was anointed of God. The Israelites wanted a king. Saul was anointed as king.

The anointing didn't change his lifestyle. On many occasions he demonstrated jealousy, vengeance; anger. On more than one occasion, he attempted to murder. And although his life was spared, it didn't change his heart from trying it again.

The anointing didn't change his personality, his behavior, his habits, his decisions, nor his choices. It changed his position in life… His job, and his ability to perform it! This he didn't even do well, and was for a lack of a better word; 'fired,' from his position and replaced with king David.

The anointing doesn't make us holy! It would have made Saul holy. It didn't!

So if we sing, preach, serve in extraordinary ways, it's the endowment of God upon our lives; not our own. Still, this will not make us holy, nor better than anyone else. It simply means we're using the abilities given to us by God for His service.

The anointing doesn't build our kingdom… It builds God's!

We must stop lowering what we think, what we've been taught and believe are the ways of God; to our own levels, and measure up with the truth of His word. Yes, we dance, we fall out, we run the pews. It's emotions! It's the expression of our feelings towards God! It has no bearing whatsoever on us being holy or anointed of God.

Emotions won't bring us freedom… Obedience will! The emotions will come as a result of our decision to surrender ourselves to God; which leads us to freedom. Emotions without surrender, will cause our lives to remain in the same place, no matter how many times we cry out. We must surrender to obtain freedom!

Holiness; is our lives set aside for the service of God. It's not an act. It's a lifestyle. A lifestyle is our behavior, our choices; our sacrifices we make to live a life pleasing to God, evident of the fruits that we bear.

The Anointing of God endows us with the ability to serve in some capacity; with the ability to draw or attract others to these abilities… To lead them to God! Nothing in there had much to do with us, but rather our lives, and endowed abilities to lead others to God. In simpler terms… The anointing isn't about us! It's God making us more than we are to bring attention back to Him… Not us!

Holiness is not a performance! The anointing doesn't change our character one bit! The Anointing of God are tools which God equips us with to build His Kingdom.

We see the emotions without the change. We've grown accustomed and satisfied with it. All of the phrases come with it… 'Oh church was really great!' 'The spirit was really high today!' Yet no change! We've grown to enjoy this type of service because… It moves us emotionally and doesn't change us spiritually! We feel good without the need to, or the pressure to change. This feeds our emotions, yet leaves us spiritually bankrupt.

Lest we be confused! Lest any of us Boast!

God said this to me a day after He gave me this writing to describe us… "It's like waxing a car with an empty tank. You put on a nice shine, but you don't go anywhere!"

GOD IS GOING TO GIVE YOU WEALTH

I open my hands to receive money. I open my mind to ideas, suggestions, direction from You; wisdom of God. I have yielded my vessel to You, to make room in my heart to receive wealth by showing me the purpose of wealth. Wealth isn't to buy me things. Wealth isn't for me to have the best of everything. Those are the residuals of wealth. The purpose of wealth is to bless others. The purpose of wealth is to invest in the lives of others. Wealth gives us opportunities to be a part of lives that we wouldn't have had the chance to be. Wealth allows us to be the Hands of God to bless others. It gives opportunity for others to honor His generosity through us. Wealth allows us to take our place in society. It

MY NAME IS LOVE

allows us to show the world that gain can be obtained without greed, without stepping over others; without manipulation!

As Christians, we should pray about telling a congregation of people that God is going to bless them with wealth! We mislead when we do that. So many of us aren't prepared to receive wealth. Wealth would only run us away from God; as our hearts haven't the capacity to properly receive it. This isn't wealth, it's riches. Riches would only make us more of who we already are inside. We would do wrong things. Buy frivolous things!

We would be like the servant given only one talent, and asked to give an account of it when his master returned. He would find emptiness. He would find no investment in the lives of anyone but ours. He would find no investment in ventures to increase the riches, and restructure it into wealth. He would find no business plan, no blueprint for success. He would find only squandering and selfishness. He would find no investment in lives; no champion of causes. This is not the purpose of wealth.

Why would we tell a people ill prepared for wealth that God is going to give them something they're not prepared to receive! This only gets people excited; which leads them to disappointment.

God doesn't tell someone they're going to be a doctor unless they have that desire, and are mentally able and adequate to attend medical school. You're telling something to someone who's looking for money to fall out of the sky. Not someone prepared to receive it through hard work, commitment; through subtle words from God deposited in our minds through ideas and suggestions.

We dismiss these leads as passing thoughts in our minds. We have no idea that God uses people, or anything He chooses; to birth His plans within us. We don't accept these things because we're ill prepared. We destroy the seed, through ideas; that wealth was to come to us through. So we look for it in all the wrong places. Like through lottery tickets, gambling and other means God never intended us to venture into.

We want it now! We want it today! We don't want the pleasure of working with God; growing and passing on to others what we've learned. We want it to fall out of the sky, our ship to come in, or somehow we stumble upon wealth. It doesn't work like that!

And now we see why we've wrongly been told that we're going to receive wealth when we were no ways near prepared. We neither had the capacity for wealth, nor the right reasons and uses for it. We neither had the drive, determination and the ability to listen and act upon the ideas God places in our hearts and minds to gravitate us towards wealth.

If God tells you you're going to have wealth… He'll first remove wrong things from your heart to make room; the capacity, for you to receive it. This comes through yielding and surrendering to the ways of God. This comes through asking for directions and guidance through prayer and meditation. This comes through recognizing the move of God; in both subtle, and in non conventional ways. Here; we're sensitive to gentle nudges from God to do something, or to move in a certain direction.

People don't want to do all of these things! They just want riches handed to them with little or no effort. They disqualify themselves from receiving wealth from God. His ways! His reasons!

I know from personal experience how God prepares a heart to receive wealth. He removes junk and foolishness. Through a life surrendered to Him, He removes selfish desires and replaces them with His desires. You now want what He wants for your life.

A desire for some nice things stay, but they're no longer your priority. They come to you as a residual to the wealth you obtain; to walk in the purpose of God to touch lives. This is the reason God gives wealth. Not to accumulate things!

God gives us wealth to be His hands to others. Not to fill our own pockets!

If God gave you a million dollar idea… Would you sit on it? We want riches handed to us without effort!

Oh the experiences, the journeys, and the wisdom we would forfeit!

WE KNOW HOW TO SEEM SPIRITUAL… BUT WE DON'T KNOW HOW TO LIVE

We want the power of God, but ignore the basics that gives us character. We focus on title and position rather than integrity.

Being spiritual is not the 'woo woo woo'… It's a life lived separately from the world where others see us as Light and Salt. Not by our words, but by our lifestyles!

Loudness is a false negative to distract you from my real agenda. I'm really small, hurting; damaged inside. I come off strong, but I'm really not. My loudness is my extended arm to keep you from discovering how damaged I really am inside. It's really a cry for help, as I hate being who I am. But I don't know how to free myself!

The Bible says… "But those things which proceed out of the mouth come from the heart, and they defile a man." Matthew 15:18 So I act out what's truly in my heart. Like; start an argument to get out the house. Start a phony argument so I can leave in a false rage, to see my side chick. Like making you feel guilty while I do dirt. You're left wondering; what just happened, and what did I do. You're left to sit in guilt while I'm out having fun; doing wrong.

HELP US LORD

A loud voice is a mirror. Just like our personality… Whatever is in me, I reflect it onto you. Because I don't see much in myself, I reflect that onto you through guilt, shame and put downs. I have to see good in myself to reflect good onto others. If my self esteem is low; that's what those closest to me will receive from me. And it comes through my voice!

Because I'm torn down inside, ill tear you down! Misery loves company. The Bible tells us clearly that… "Death and Life are in the power of the tongue." Proverbs 18:21 This is a principle of God which we can no longer afford to ignore. The other part of that principle is… "As a man speaks, so is he." A man speaks life or death; uplift or ruin from his mouth!

God said to me this day… "We know how to seem spiritual; but we don't know how to live!" It's time we learn the basic principles of God.

THEY WERE STILL SLAVES AFTER THEY WERE FREE

Four hundred years as slaves. Generations born into bondage; died in bondage. They multiplied so, that the Egyptians feared the sheer number of them. The people of God cried out for deliverance. But were they really free after they received it!

In modern translation; these weren't the people of the world who didn't know God. This was the seed of Abraham. Seed of the promise of multiplicity from God. Yet they were slaves for 400 years.

Today we would say… 'No way would I be a slave again once I was set free! You'd have to be crazy to want to be a slave again!' Would you? Really!

The Israelites cried unto God for a deliverer. Moses was spared at birth, raised in the ways and house of the most powerful man on Earth. Even

MY NAME IS LOVE

before his birth; the Sovereignty of God chose him to deliver His people from centuries of bondage.

The time came. God, through the hand of Moses, set the children of Israel free. Free to worship God. Freedom from their taskmasters. Freedom from their labors.

Moses would quickly discover this very essential truth… Their bondage may have ended, but they were still slaves. They no longer had the shackles and whips; yet they still were not free!

Where a man travels, so does his heart and mind. They're inseparable! The Israelites had the desire for freedom, but lacked the understanding of it!

Many times they cried out… "Take us back to Egypt! We were better off with the Egyptians as slaves! Did you set us free only to leave us to die in the desert!" They murmured! They complained! They criticized Moses.

They were ungrateful and hard headed. They lacked the knowledge that… Gratitude and complaint can't abide in the same atmosphere. Although they saw miracles daily by the Hand of God, they still complained.

They got off track. They built false idols after knowing God was their god. They wandered in the wilderness needlessly. They died off! Many never seeing the promise.

This sounds horrible when we hear it. And we swear this could never be us today! No! We may not be in physical bondage… But are we really free!

We have exchanged the physical bondage for the mental bondage! Just as the Israelites had a deliverer, so do we today. Moses has been exchanged for Christ!

Christ; through salvation, delivered us from the slavery of sin. The analogies run parallel. We, the people of God today, can be set free; but still not enjoy the benefits of freedom.

The Israelites were the chosen people of God, yet they lived in carnality. They weren't pleasing God with their lives. They acted up so much, that it moved God from correcting them; to punishment. They filled their void of freedom with the wrong things.

When someone is set free from bondage, they're at liberty to be bound to something else. The Bible tells us this… "You have been set free from sin and have become slaves to righteousness."

In clearer words… Being a slave to righteousness makes us free in our lives! The problem being that once Christ set some of us free, we didn't make that transition to Righteousness. We remained in the wilderness as babes! We forfeited our freedom by holding on to our lives; instead of fully releasing them to Christ!

A life not fully committed to Christ is not free. Jesus said in John 8:31-36, "If you hold to my teaching, you are really my disciples. Then you will know the truth, and the Truth will set you free."

The Bible also tells us this… "So if the Son sets you free, you will be free indeed." John 8:36 Jesus sets us free to righteousness. But if we don't fill that vacuum of freedom we obtain from Christ with the pursuit of righteousness… It will be filled with the world.

The truth is this… No matter the bondage, if we don't replace our mentality with something good; productive and positive… Something else will enslave us! Life abhors a vacuum. It will seek to fill the space.

So we say… 'No way I'd be a slave today!' Then we must ask ourselves; what have we filled the vacuum with after Christ set us free through salvation! Have we filled it with righteousness, and a life surrendered to Christ. Or have we left it not filled at all.

The Israelites filled their freedom with things; instead of God. They allowed their freedom to become no more than a Rescue! They replaced their physical slavery with a mental slavery; just in another geographical place. They said they wanted freedom, but what most of them really wanted; was a Rescue! They had gone from being slaves to the Egyptians... To being slaves to themselves!

We must ask ourselves today... Are we any different after God saved us through salvation! Have we stayed on our path of righteousness seeking Christ, or have we wandered through the wilderness in our own ways again.

Did we truly want the Freedom that Christ provides through a surrendered life. Or did we only want a Rescue from the situation we were in!

If we continue on the path seeking righteousness; we truly wanted freedom. If we turned away; back to our ways... We were just looking to be rescued.

This is where we discover... We may have been set free from bondage! Yet; we're still a slave!

~ A SPECIAL WRITING TO ME~

Years ago, when I first moved here, this is the writing I shared with a congregation. This is the writing the young lady moved out of her seat to meet me in the aisle to ask me... "Can I have a copy of that!" It's the writing that became... "The Woman In The Aisle."

This special young lady showed me that day how people must have moved towards Jesus when they needed something from Him. Tired of being sick! Sick of being tired; they were lowered through rooftops, pressed through the crowds. They climbed trees to get near Him. They used any method; any means they could to get to Jesus. Unashamed, all pride aside; not in the least embarrassed… They pursued Him with vigor to be healed, released; to be set free and renewed.

This special young lady showed me that day, how that must have been. It was a Beautiful thing to see, and to be a part of… The move of God touching lives!

STUCK IN SOME PLACES

Looking over my life, I see that I've been stuck in some places. Through maturity, I never want to re-visit those places. It's not a hard thing to do to get stuck in places. Sometimes the worst of life hits us, and it's hard to recover. Sometimes grief and sorrow overtake us, and we can't find our ways out of them.

The hurt of a broken marriage, or relationship can ruin us if we don't seek help. The loss of a loved one can be tremendous. These losses can be devastating and life altering.

Through tremendous pain and turmoil, we can find our personalities lacking and our self esteem diminished. Our confidence can be shattered when we've invested all we had into something, or someone that used or abandoned us. The emotional anguish can be exhausting!

We can find ourselves alone, humiliated, unwilling and unable to trust others. We seek isolation rather than company; to be alone with our grief. We've become a shell of the person we once were.

MY NAME IS LOVE

Diminished self esteem, lack of self confidence, and self worth, are not only recipes for disaster; they can also become a recipe for success if given to God. Handled alone, we can eat our way to temporary comfort. We can shop away our troubles; only to meet them at the door when we arrive home. We can become bitter, and mad at the world, if we hold on to these things.

We can search to dull our conscience with alcohol, drugs or worse. These are only band aids; not solutions. The only remedy is seeking help; If we're not spiritually strong enough. If we're emotionally able; we can turn these issues over to God.

For those of you in judgment, I've been to the place where I wasn't strong enough or willing to turn my issues over to God. My trust in Him diminished. If I didn't seek professional help then, I might not be around to tell you about it today.

Pain which leads to emotional conditions are nothing to take lightly. Get help and pray also. God gives us professionals to help us in these areas too. By turning these areas over to God, we're saying we're fed up with living with the weights and baggage that comes with our disappointments in life. Asking God to heal us of these conditions; is our first step to freedom. Asking Him to heal us from the bad habits we've obtained like eating, smoking, drinking or whatever is our next step.

By asking Him; those desires will eventually fall off. Hate them if necessary, and ask God to take them from you. You won't have the strength; but He will! If you find yourself still in love with these things; ask Him to allow you to hate that thing.

Desire is the key element in continuing something. The desire must be dealt with, or it will remain.

One of the most important steps is forgiveness. Forgiving ourselves for where we find ourselves, and forgiving those that hurt us. Without this essential element; we can not be free. We'll be bound by bitterness, which will destroy us internally; and mask itself on us externally by our attitudes, our personalities and our appearance.

Forgiveness is simply an act of our will to let go of the hurt, the pain and the disappointment. Forgiveness is between us and God alone. We don't even need to seek out those that wronged us, and let them know we've forgiven them. This is between us and God.

Besides; they'll see the difference in your smile, your attitude and even the way you carry yourself. You're no longer stuck, but lifted up to walk in your light that God has placed within you. You're now a witness, and have a tremendous testimony. It's not what you've done, but what God has done for you!

Your days of self loathing and defeat are over. You've become alive again, breathing the breath of God within your lungs. You've been wounded; but now your wounds have mended with the salve of the Great Physician. He's healed you to live, and to touch the lives of others. You're alive now!

You're stuck no more!

GOD DELIGHTS IN BROKEN VESSELS

If God were to go to the store shopping for containers or vessels of water; He would shop for very specific ones for His use. He wouldn't pick the pretty shiny ones, full of glamour; the ones only used for display or when company arrives. He would pick the plain and simple ones. The broken vessels; yet fit for His use.

MY NAME IS LOVE

Thank God we are not God. We would pass right by the junk and go for the glamour.

God delights in broken vessels! For most likely they're cracked and leak. He loves the kind that leak, because they've been emptied of their contents. They're empty; ready to be filled with new water. Patching them isn't a problem. His gentle hands mend and repair all areas.

These once broken; now usable vessels are fit for the Master's use. They're ready to be poured into, and filled to overflowing; with His Living Water. The Master takes great pride in these vessels. They become His favorites. He uses them often. For they are willing to be emptied; and filled again.

They aren't like the shiny, pretty ones; that were so afraid of being broken... That they remained on their shelves; full of their own content. Only looking good; but of no use to the Master.

The vessel often used; was once a shiny, pretty one. One day it grew tired of not being used by the Master. It took a leap of faith off the shelf to gain its Master's attention. It fell to the ground; shattered and broken into pieces.

The Master recognized it's faith, and immediately went to work on putting it back together. It was stronger now! The glue the Master used to mend it; was infinite in strength. It lost it's contents when it fell. The Master filled it with special water... Holy and Pure!

This would now be it's mission in life... To fill other's cups with the Master's water. It could no longer be full of itself to do this. So it always sought to be empty; so it could enjoy the constant filling by the Master.

Be empty vessels, and be filled continuously with the living water of the Master. Be full of yourself; and remain of no use to the Master... Collecting dust upon your shelf!

THROUGH WHOSE EYES ARE YOU SEEN

To Joseph's brothers he was a pest, a spoiled brat; a dreamer and a usurper of their inheritance, position and place in the family.

To God... He was Zaphnapaneah; Governor of all Egypt! He was the right hand to the Pharaoh! Second most powerful man on Earth! He was keeper of the grain, and savior of countless lives!

Joseph neither wanted, nor cared about his family inheritance. His heart and eyes were on something much larger than a family inheritance. Through his dreams, he saw deeper, larger; broader.

His inheritance would encompass millions. Because of his inheritance; his brothers would live to see theirs. In what would have been a grain-less time; Joseph was life to the very brothers that sought to kill him, betrayed him, and sold him as a slave.

There would come a time in his brothers lives when they would see him as he truly was in God; regardless of his rank, title and position in the family inheritance. God bypassed, and ranked him outside of his family title; to a position so high... That everyone had to bow to him. Even his brothers! Even his parents! Only Pharaoh was higher than him.

"Here comes that dreamer;" said his brothers! No! Here stands Second in Command, Savior of Lives; Perpetuator and Hand of the Promise of God to Abraham.

Through whose eyes are you seen?

GIVE US LOVE LORD

Give us the capacity to love Lord!
The hearts to display it; The ability to understand it;
The wisdom to receive it;
The desire to promote it;
The consistency to commit to it;
The energy to seek it… The need to want it prevalent in our lives.

Give us love Lord!
The ability to see You; The comprehension to understand You;
The knowledge to appreciate You;
The yearning to express You as light, as joy; as care & concern for others
through our beings.

Give us love Lord!
You are both Source & Author Lord.
Apart from You, can we fully understand it;
Attempt to display it; Comprehend how to receive it;
Understand its limits and express its depths.

Can we see it with gratitude;
Appreciate it with humility.
Can we Express it without measure.

Without You Lord, it mystifies us;
It eludes us;
It's a dream we cannot fathom.

May we yield our hearts for capacity;
May we broaden our minds for expansion;
May we yield our beings for giving;
May we heed our resources for gifting.

HELP US LORD

Love remains in expression;
It displays in fullness;
It seeks no limits;
It has no borders.

Love is free!
The gift from God;
It was never earned or rewarded;
It just is;

Unstoppable; Immeasurable;
Accountable;
Durable & Dependable; Impeccable;
Reliable;
Capable;
Justifiable;
Irreplaceable!

Each of these words describes the characteristics of Love. Each of them end with the word 'Able.'

Love is synonymous with Able. Able is the description; and character of God!

Give us love Lord!

HERE COMES THAT DREAMER

Are we the dreamer or the brothers?

There's a season that will manifest your destiny. Until then… No matter how much you try, strive or even try to do good; it will still come in the time appointed of God. Walk in integrity anyways.

The Bible tells us of Joseph's success in the big things. It mentions nothing of his trials; of his humanity, or the struggles he had to bring himself to excellence. There was a place where he had to decide that no matter what, or regardless of his situation; he was going to walk in excellence before God.

This wasn't an easy task. Betrayed by his brothers! Forfeiting his freedom as a slave! Having his character attacked as a man of integrity; that he worked so hard to build. And lied on by his bosses wife, and innocently thrown into prison.

I don't care what anyone says, that's a lot to recover from! It's easy for us to read his story with ease from a distance, but he had to live it; wondering if his dream from God would ever come to pass.

The dreams of God rarely manifest in fields of daisies; but through suffering!

Suffering leaves us with the gift of Humility… To perform the work of God; not our own!

TO WHICH VOICE DO YOU LISTEN

Joseph was told he was a slave in Egypt. His spirit and his heart told him he was so much more. He was the man God showed him in his dreams. Time, preparation and experience; would have to catch up with him to reveal this truth. His circumstances didn't ruin him; they honed him. His experiences didn't deter him; they prepared him for greatness. He didn't wait to be promoted to walk in Excellence. Walking in Excellence is what guided him to his promotion!

He listened to the voice of who his dreams from God told him he was… Not his circumstances!

WASN'T OURS TO CHANGE

Your goal shouldn't be to rescue a bad man for you to feel needed. Someone to eventually exhaust you and spend you. Your goal should be to partner and support a good man, so the both of you can change life around you.

It's within the nature of a woman to help; to nurture. But she's misplacing those skills today in the wrong men to puff herself up with pride believing that she's a savior. She's not! A woman is a multiplier; not a savior. There's only One of those named Jesus.

A woman multiplies what's given to her. If she takes in and accepts a bad man, she'll naturally try to multiply him. What she'll find is that she neither has the strength, nor the skills for foolishness. In her stubborn attempts to fix him; she fails to realize that he's exhausted her, and emptied her treasure for the good man who was assigned to come into her life.

Now she's spent, bitter and guarded. She failed to realize that God only, is capable of changing any of our hearts. At best, she may only manipulate a man into a performance; rather than a true change. He may act liked he changed just for your silence. Whenever you're not around, he reverts back to his old self; because true change is only within the privy of God.

You can't change yourself without God, so how do we think you can change anyone. All women today must grasp and take hold of this revelation knowledge given to us by God.

God is restructuring our views and perceptions of marriage to align with the truth. God is taking back His institution of marriage. It was never ours to manipulate! But it's just like us to change something so we don't have to obey the rules. It's our nature! We as Christian's; our nature has been changed. Therefore, we should be doing better than the world in our marriages.

We don't go into worldly institutions telling them what we're going to do, and what we're not going to do. That institution of learning that you graduated from; you followed their rules, regulations and procedures, or you were removed. We're the only ones that go into God's institution and tells Him what we're going to do, and what we're not going to do. Marriage is the only institution of God that I know of. We don't know how to govern the one He's given us.

We have violated what wasn't ours to violate. We have manipulated what wasn't ours to change. We thought marriage was ours and it wasn't. It was God's all along. We were only privileged participants to enter into His Institution.

THE WRONG REQUIREMENTS

What if we've been approaching and seeing marriage as wrong. What if there were requirements for entering marriage. What if we paid attention to the wrong requirements and totally ignored the real ones!

To understand this; we would have to go back to beginning and the reason for marriage to understand it's true meaning and purpose.

It began with God's first two humans; Adam and Eve. Being they were the first humans created by God; they didn't date each other. When a man sees a woman for the first time and these are the first words out of his mouth… "And Adam said, This is now bone of my bones, and flesh of my flesh: she shall be called Woman, because she was taken out of Man." Genesis 2:23 This isn't to date her! They were life's first couple; life's first husband and wife.

HELP US LORD

It was six days, God created the Heavens and the Earth back then. It was all done in order. It's the only way God does things. So it was with His first couple. Their relationship was in order. It fell up under one of God's first institutions called marriage.

Marriage would be the parameters of God's relationship between a man and a woman for the creation of love and the family. This would be the place the two became one.... Where they walked within structure and compliance. God designed one way in, and one way out. The original exit that God designed for marriage was the death of one of the participants.

God designed marriage as the place the couple would meet and fulfill all of their needs... Emotionally, physically, sexually and spiritually. The marriage would be the place to focus on meeting each other's needs; not having the distraction of more than one person in their lives. It's a union of two.

Within this structure, is an umbrella. An umbrella protects us from the elements; a covering! This is where the couple would find protection from the elements of the world; by remaining under their covering. This is where the family would be structured, reared, raised and one day released to have families of their own. It was God's original plan for marriage. It's His plan today.

With any institution, there are rules and requirements. You don't enter without first meeting the requirements of the institution. Marriage is no different. It's just that no one ever told us this. Or it's that we were given the wrong requirements for acceptance into this institution.

These are the requirements we've been told for the entrance into the Institution of Marriage. First we needed a ring; an engagement ring and later a wedding ring. The woman would require a wedding dress. She would sometimes spend thousands of dollars on it, and wear it for only one day of her life. The institution would require a marriage license; to cover any legal obligations. A certificate of marriage would be provided afterwards, as proof of entrance into the institution. A reception; a place to congregate and celebrate would normally be conducted. A honeymoon would be the icing on the cake; (oh by the way, I forgot to mention a cake would also be required), to consummate the relationship between the two. This would be a sign of their love, devotion and commitment to only each other for the remainder of their lives.

With any Institution, there's an entrance exam. This exam determines if you qualify to enter this distinguished foundation. The Institution of Marriage also has an entrance examination, and requirements that no one ever told us before. They told us all about the requirements for the ceremony; but never an exam was required to enter the marriage.

Marriage is the Institution created by God for a husband and wife to join, commit, love and relate. It's the place God intended to form our families. If this is the Institution of God, then God would establish the rules for entrance.....Being that it's His; not ours. If we enter something, it's something we want, and we must meet the requirements for entry.

Here is God's entrance examination for His Institution of Marriage. This one is called Relocation; Leave and Cleave... "For this reason a man will leave his father and mother and be united to his wife, and the two will become one flesh." Genesis 2:24 A man must leave his father and mother to join life together with his wife.

This one is called Spiritual Compatibility... "Do not be yoked together with unbelievers. For what do righteousness and wickedness have in common? Or what fellowship can light have with darkness?" 2 Corinthians 6:14 This scripture tells us that we should marry someone that's spiritually compatible to us. This doesn't mean someone who just says they're a Christian; but two people that bear the fruit of it through their lifestyles. If not; you're going to have trouble!

Here, the example of marriage was compared to the agricultural term 'yoked.' Yoked was the process of placing two working farm animals in a wooden device. There they'd be connected together and move together jointly; as one! It was an example of how closely related the husband and wife would be in marriage. The Bible even says…"The two become one flesh." It's the closest relationship on Earth! No other relationship on Earth compares to the marriage relationship.

This one is the hardest, and most misunderstood parts of the entrance examination. It's the one most people lie on in the exam. Upfront they agree to this requirement; but after they enter the institution… They fail to keep their promise!

This requirement is called Order and Purpose. God does nothing without order, structure and purpose. It's only fitting that the Institution of God would have high standards for anything associated with Him. These are His requirements for both husband and wife on how to relate to one another within the bonds of marriage… "Husbands, love your wives, just as Christ loved the church and gave himself up for her." "Wives, submit to your husbands as to the Lord. For the husband is the head of the wife as Christ is the head of the church, his body, of which he is the Savior. In this same way, husbands ought to love their wives as their own bodies. "He who loves his wife loves himself." Ephesians 5:25

This is the most disqualifying part of the examination. This is where many fail to come to terms with, and align themselves with the institution. So they lie on the examination! They agree during the indoctrination process; with no intentions of fulfilling the requirements after they've been accepted into the institution.

MY NAME IS LOVE

The truth is… If we can't meet this requirement for marriage; we disqualify ourselves for entrance. Remember, marriage is not our institution; it's Gods! To enter something that belongs to Him; requires us to go by His rules for entrance.

The truth is, so many of us enter God's institution disqualified every day, and then we wonder why our marriages fail. We've got to wake up and do better!

What we've always thought of as the hardest requirement; was actually the most beautiful and liberating one of them all! Submission from man or woman has nothing to do with weakness at all! Only the strong submit themselves to God; husband and wife. Weakness rebels; does it's own things, and remains out of order.

We must truly ask ourselves this question before marriage… Can I submit myself, my will and my desires to God for this man or woman! If the answer is no; that's not the right person for you. It's a pre-test we never give ourselves before we enter.

But we must start today; not tomorrow! If there's no man or woman that we can submit our lives, will and desire unto God to… Then marriage isn't for us! Because these are the requirements of God for entry into His Institute.

If we never knew there were requirements to enter into God's Institution of Marriage… We do now, and we are no longer without excuse! No more excuses!

HELP US LORD

CAN'T DIFFERENTIATE

Today, many women can't differentiate that a man that's being nice, isn't weak. He's just being nice! When did being nice start equating to weakness.

I love nice people. They're the kind I want around me. I don't like drama and can't stand nonsense. It's a backwards world and a backwards mentality that what we use to label as a gentleman; is wrongly misnomered as soft.

The fault is not in the man... But in the woman that see's him as such. She fails to appreciate what could be good for her. She fails to understand what could be lasting and secure; providing her a future. She fails to see with such a man, she would properly fit in as a lady, woman and wife... And within; would find her purpose for being.

She fails to see because she limits. She mislabels and misunderstands truth. She has placed her belief in a lie, and therefore her vision and understanding is skewed. As a result, her choices are misaligned and off kilter. She chooses wrong instead of right for her, as the foundation of her decision making is out of balance.

Each time she chooses wrong, the walls around her heart get higher and thicker. She becomes hard, callous and a shadow of what she once was. She doesn't want to be this person. This is who she had to become from making wrong choices; in pain producing relationships.

She was not made for such! She was created by God to be loved, receive love and express love in a safe environment. But she lacked the wisdom and insight to distinguish between the good man and the bad.

She and many others were wrongly led to believe that nice was weak; and kind was soft. She failed to see and realize that angels come to us

MY NAME IS LOVE

unaware, and some of them are in the form and shape of a good man… Given a strong heart to love and care for a woman as he was designed to do by God. But her foolishness misjudged him, mislabeled him; misunderstood him, because he didn't come rough, rude and selfish. He appeared in a different form.

He appeared as a man… Responsible, reliable; dependable! He was kind and trustworthy! These qualities God refined in him. He appeared to you; after he was now ready to display them… To walk in them!

But you rejected him as less than! When he was so much more than you would ever need in life. He was your future. He was your savior from foolishness and heartache. He was a true man strengthened and hardened by God through the fires of dross removing. He came to you and appeared humbled, because he successfully graduated from God's School of Humility. It's the only way he can be now. He's learned through hardness and awareness; that God requires him to see and treat a woman only one way… As a gift from God.

A man isn't at fault for being kind. It takes character to be kind. This is not a deficit. It was a deficit in your character not his. He was lined up where he was supposed to be in God, exhibiting the fruits of the Spirit by being kind.

He came prepared to treat you as such. Through your blindness, you mislabeled, misunderstood and rejected him. Now he is the answer to the prayer for another woman who appreciates and cherishes him.

Don't miss out due to blindness!

NOW I SEE

They were the words spoken to me from God through prophesy over 30 years ago… "I will speak to you like Moses!"

Today, I truly understood those words God spoke to me so long ago. He speaks to me at His pleasure, and I write what He speaks as His scribe. But today was different.

Today I saw something totally different when I went to my room to pray. With the enlightenment, I immediately got up off my knees in amazement and listened to what God was saying to me.

I had known that God had referenced my purpose to Moses before. Moses was a deliverer. I knew God would use the writings He gives me to set us free today. But we're not slaves in bondage you say! Yes we are! We're slaves to ourselves, residing in our own self erected prisons from living far beneath the truth.

I now see what God is doing. No, we aren't physical slaves like the Israelites. Our slavery as the people of God today is… We live too close to the world! It's not about proximity. It's about spirituality. We as Christians today look no different; act no different than those in the world. Yes, we may try to on Sunday at church; but what about the rest of the week! Our lifestyles blend, rather than stand out. We've even taken the world into the church, instead of the church taking the world out of us!

So what is God doing to correct this? He's giving us truth! He's giving it to us; not in parables, but in a manner that's easily understood by all of us. He's going back to the basics to get all of us back on track. He's weeding out the mistruths and misconceptions that we thought were right, and replacing them with truth.

Once we hear; we're accountable and responsible. No more excuses. No more… 'I didn't know!' It's lining up time, and God is lining us up with the truth.

Why is He doing this? The Bible says… "Christ will return for His bride without spot or wrinkle." Ephesians 5:27 He's getting the wrinkles and spots out of His bride. And just like Moses lead the millions of Israelites from the bondage of slavery from the Egyptians; God is leading us back to truth and accountability. There will be a great leading of us out of; and away from the world as we should have been all along. One will be light and salt to the other as it should be. Christian marriages will be light to those in the world, instead of the divorce rates being the same.

We have allowed the world to tell us what was cool, hip and right. We've been over influenced by their ways and attitudes. We've adopted their dress and mannerisms; even their communication. They have influenced the way we live our lives, rather than us having influence over theirs.

The worst kind of slave is the one that doesn't realize he's in bondage. He's a slave; yet he sees the world as fine around him. It's the cry of the blind… "Didn't we say to you in Egypt, 'Leave us alone; let us serve the Egyptians'? It would have been better for us to serve the Egyptians than to die in the desert!" Exodus 14:12

God is once again, like Moses, leading us away from our bondage. This time not from the Egyptians… But from the world and ourselves. He's not leading us to die in the wilderness, but to live in the light of His magnificence.

He will lead and deliver us… With Truth!

HELP US LORD

DEFIANCE

Something that we've long forgotten is… God is a God of Order!

He does nothing without reason and purpose. He set the Universe in order. It's how the Sun, Moon and Seasons serve us. It's the order of God.

The opposite of Order is Chaos! The dictionary defines chaos as… 'Complete disorder and confusion.' This describes many marriages today. Marriage is an institution created by God to work in order; just as the Sun, Moon and Seasons.

Time is consistent. Each day for thousands of years it's worked the same way. We count on time in our lives for its consistency. It never fails us. It will always be just where it's supposed to be now and always. Time is an example of the Order of God. It's not one way one day; and different the next. It's the same always, and will always remain in its place; dependable, reliable, trustworthy; consistent.

God's plan for our marriages is no different than any of His other Laws and Institutions. He expects them to follow the Order He ordained over them. The difference between Laws and Institutions are… Laws are set in place established by God to perform the same way consistently. They're governed by the invisible. The institution of marriage involves two individuals with wills of their own; who before marriage, agreed to govern those wills, and walk in alignment with the rules of marriage. This is what we vow to in marriage… To govern our wills and tendencies! The difference… All things obey God except man!

No one is forced into marriage. It's a voluntary agreement. The two know the rules before they enter. They confirm their vows during the ceremony. But why do still so many fail!

MY NAME IS LOVE

Death is the reason! We want to live; rather than die to ourselves. Our nerve endings jump off, and we want to please them rather than to remain in place. We want a buffet; when we only signed up for one item. We lose something called contentment, and believe we're missing out on the things others are doing; and the foolishness we see on TV. We starve the marriage with arguing, fighting and nonsense; rather than feed it with love and devotion. We look for ways out; instead of solutions. We focus on the small, and lose sight of the larger vision. Where there was once Order, we've now allowed in chaos!

Sure we grow and change in life, but the preview we gave someone while dating, and the engagement phase; we owe them that person and better! This is who we promised to be!

Men, we fail when we now think we have a maid; instead of a wife. Yes it's wonderful when wives do things for her husband; but a man should show appreciation, and reciprocate by also helping. She was 'honey' and 'baby' while dating; now pride and defiance enters in and he can't express his feelings and emotions. He's too cool to show softness. He's fooled into believing that being a man is not showing his feelings. He lessens the value of the treasure he once found; and stands before him.

'I'm gonna be me,' he now states! Rather than remain dead; he's become alive. He walks in defiance to the Order established by God… To love his wife as the Bible commands… "Husbands, love your wives, just as Christ loved the church and gave himself up for her. " His command from God, and the one that he voluntarily agreed to before marriage; was to love this woman so much that he would even give his life for her if he had to. That's the same love displayed by Christ!

A woman is a Multiplier! God made her to give back more than she's given. She's given a seed; she produces life through a child. This is a beautiful thing, but the principle can also be used negatively.

HELP US LORD

A man builds a house, the woman makes it a home. He brings home groceries, she makes a meal. Whatever he brings her… She multiplies! If he brings her love, she multiplies it and it becomes romance. If he brings her nonsense, she's gonna multiply that too with her words and her attitude. A man shouldn't push his wife to be something she wasn't created by God to be. He should lead her to love, not push her towards having to defend herself. You water a delicate flower, talk kindly to it; and place it in its light to be nourished.

The Bible gives a woman a template for a successful marriage as a wife in Proverbs 31. This woman walks in the Order God established for her marriage. Because her husband loved her, she multiplied it and "did him good; not evil all the days of his life." Her good was multiplied into praise from her husband and children. With the devotion she received from her husband, she encouraged him in praise, which multiplied into his confidence to take his place in his career and in society.

These are the beautiful things a woman does in marriage when she walks in the Order God has ordained. But there are some that walk out of order into chaos. They do this by defiance. Instead of being dead, they want to be alive! Control takes the place of cooperation. Attitude takes the place of praise. Instead of multiplying good; now negativity is multiplied through blame and criticism.

'I'll take over'… She states silently in her mind! I'll use control and manipulation through withholding love and affection to get what I want. I'll put him down; criticize him and belittle him as a man. Instead of speaking sweet to him, I'll fuss and argue with him. He'll never win; because my mind runs circles around his. Where he thinks of one thing, I think of many. I'll win every time, because he's confused or lacks the ability to keep up with me verbally. I'll overwhelm him into silence.'

This is not the woman he dated and agreed to marry. This is someone else that he doesn't recognize! It's not that she can't be different, she doesn't want to be. It's defiance! She listens to the foolishness of her single friends telling her... 'Don't put up with him! You need to just leave him! I wouldn't listen to him!' They care not if they ruin her marriage. It's a dangerous place to give poor advice to marriages.

She's made up her mind; this is who she wants to, or has to be. She's used her building skills to demolish. Unfortunately, she's good at this too!

Love can be such a beautiful thing when two people respect and cherish each other. No time for games and foolishness; just moving forward in love. Why is that so hard to do!

It's a mindset! If the two would just make up their minds to do these things; to be these things to each other... It would be an incredible relationship! But pride enters in; and we listen to our lesser natures, and we slip in our standards.

Strength allows us to push pride away; and be these things we need to be for ourselves, and for our marriage. We must first be these things for ourselves; before we can be them for someone else. If you can't control your behavior single; you definitely won't control it married! You'll need even more strength; living with someone, and adapting to a new lifestyle.

If you already know this will be a problem for you; don't drag someone else's life into your shortcomings! If you lack discipline; don't like order and cooperating... Marriage isn't the place to be!

The Bible tells us... "A wise woman builds her home, but a foolish woman tears it down with her own hands." Proverbs 14:1

Without cooperation it won't work. Unless she buys into the plan of God; it won't work! The man can lead all he wants. The home and marriage will be in disarray, if she refuses to follow, and to be led of

God. The Bible tells us in Ephesians… "However, each one of you also must love his wife as he loves himself, and the wife must respect her husband." Ephesians 5:22

Why was this stated in the Bible? Because it's a death reminder! It's a reminder of the yardstick God laid before us in marriage! It's a reminder that at times, our flesh, mind and mouth goes rogue; and must be brought back into alignment. It's the nature of the flesh to rebel, to be defiant… It's why our vows are to God, not to each other. And our love is based on our commitments; rather than our feelings!

The once confident man is now confused; searching to find his place in his home and in life. She could build him up; she's a multiplier. She can also tear him down. She walks in opposition to whom God created her to be. She finds no peace in her life. None of us will; walking outside of the will of God, and who we were created to be.

God created Order to govern His Universe and His families. If we decide to enter His institution of marriage; we must husband and wife; govern ourselves to the Order of His commands in love; not defiance!

BLIND & BACKWARDS

I once heard a woman say… "If a man can tell me what to do, then he can tell me what to do!"

Marriage isn't about telling each other what to do! We're not children! God gave us marriage to give us a person that has our best interest in mind. Someone that wants the best for us. A person to discuss our dreams, desires, our aspirations with; and to work on accomplishing them together.

MY NAME IS LOVE

A man doesn't seek to tell a woman what to do. He partners with her interdependently, and values her input in their wholeness! A woman shouldn't seek to tell a man what to do; but offers him advice from the broad spectrum of the mind God has given her.

This ain't no game! This is not a competition! It's not a heavyweight fight! Our place is not confrontational with a woman. We don't exhibit our strength by being in her face and commanding her what to do. Our position is to lead her in love; as Christ loves.

We don't take our cues from the world as Christians. We're not seeking to control our spouse. We seek to walk in the purpose of God over our lives and marriages. Women of the world will find this weak. They interpret drama as spice. Some want to be man handled. Some want to be dominant and in control.

The Bible says... "What does light have to do with darkness!" 2 Corinthians 6:14 What do the ways of the world have to do with Christian marriages? Nothing!

The world's got it all wrong. We walk in destruction when we try to mimic their lives. Come out from amongst them!

The blind can not lead the blind except they both fall in a pit.

Hearing what God is saying here, it enlightens how foolish relationships are in the world. It illuminates how far off base they are to truth, peace and progress. Nothing moves forward in constant conflict. Eyes aren't allowed to focus on truth and purpose.

A man asking for your opinion isn't weak. It's not that he doesn't have the answers. He's asking because he values you. Today, the world is backwards! If a man is decent, kind, trustworthy and reliable; even a Christian woman today, can see this type of man as weak. The bad man; they find attractive. They see for the moment, instead of for their purpose and future.

Ladies let's make this clear… You can not change a bad man to good. It's not your gift. Your gift is to enhance the potential that's already there in a good man. You have no place in the land of 'Nothing there.' This type of man will ruin you for the good God intended you to have. Your place is with 'Already there!' A man with the potential to be good for you. A man to magnify and enhance both of you; for the betterment of your lives and family.

Women wrongly believe they can change that wild bad boy and have it all. Ladies let me tell you the truth… You can't change a man! You can only manipulate him with gifts that he desires. When he has turned your gifts into trinkets… He's gone!

Change wasn't in him! You were his prey. When he devoured all he wanted, his desire is renewed; and he's now looking for his next meal. As a matter of fact, his next meal was already on his radar while he was with you.

God is the only one capable of changing any of us.

WHOSE REPORT SHALL WE BELIEVE

It's called Perspective. It's how we choose to look at; to view life. But more specifically, it's how we choose to view life happening to us.

The Bible says… "And we know that for those who love God all things work together for good, for those who are called according to his purpose." Romans 8:28 Scriptures can come with conditions to release their provisions and promises. This one applies to those who love God to relinquish its treasures. The provision is, that life as it's happening to

MY NAME IS LOVE

us; is ultimately working for our good. The good it's working towards is the refining of our natures; our character... Our spiritual growth!

Perspective is how we choose to see life and the world. Do we see it through God's eyes or our own. Wherever we find ourselves, we must choose. Better yet; it must become our lifestyles that we see things from the perspective of God. The alternative is to complain, and to look at things negatively.

Here's an example... The Israelites complained of being slaves. God sent Moses to deliver them. They still complained! They were free from 400 years of bondage. They complained!

While being led to freedom; they complained of hunger. God sent them food from the sky. They complained; instead of realizing they were being fed by the Hand of God. They were seeing miracles! They complained!

When the Egyptians pursued them, they complained; saying they were better off in Egypt as slaves. They should have rejoiced at seeing the miracle of the cloud, and fire of God from Heaven. Because of their disobedience; they wandered in the wilderness for 40 years. God had to remind them of the miracle; that neither their clothes or shoes wore out in those 40 years. Another miracle!

It's our choice to see God... Or to focus on life!

ADJUST OUR PERSPECTIVE OF RIGHT

I once heard a woman state... "I'm not built for no soft man! I talk back and I don't listen!" Let's examine this from the perspective of truth...

HELP US LORD

SOFT???

He works.
He pays his bills.
He cuts the grass.
He washes your car and his.
He comes home everyday.
He provides financially.
He has his own place.
He owns a car.
He takes care of you; the children; your children and raises them as his own.
He's present!!!
He's trustworthy!
He's calm; rarely raises his voice!
He opens doors for you.
He's kind!
He's reliable!
He's dependable!
He loves God!
He puts God first in his life!
He loves you as God commands.
He says he's a Christian.
His lifestyle and the fruits he exhibits confirm this.

Strong???

He sits at home all day playing video games while you work!
He lives with you instead of having his own place.
You pay his bills!
You pay his child support!
He still lives with his mom!
He doesn't have a job!
He's not looking for one either!

MY NAME IS LOVE

He's working on the next hookup.
He's elusive!
He comes and goes!
He's secretive!
He's sneaky!
You don't know where he is.
He's demanding!
He lies!
He's unreliable!
Not dependable!
Not a good provider!
Loud, boisterous, violent
You fear him!
Does he love your children if they aren't his.
How does he treat your children?
Is he involved in their lives or absent from them!
Does he Love or just Tolerate your children!
He says he knows God.
He wants nothing to do with God! Or only when you threaten to leave him!

This is the truth of what's going on today in our world! Sad to say; it's also in our lives as Christians!

There's nothing soft about being Dependable, Reliable & Trustworthy! We must truly open our eyes! Our perceptions must really change!

Chapter 7

TOOLS THROUGH THE WISDOM OF GOD

~God gave me the desire for her, and I thought it was love… It was Purpose! ~

We've always used our feelings as a Barometer to measure love! We've been using the wrong instrument!

OUR INTERNAL MIRRORS

The defensive will never receive help. They have removed all internal mirrors within, or covered their reflection. The problem always lies within someone else; their theme.

None of us are perfect. I've always admired those who could laugh at themselves. Those who never took themselves too seriously. People like my favorite actor; Mr. Cary Grant. Smooth, suave, handsome; he wasn't too cool to be silly. He had the confidence to laugh at himself. He had the strength to allow us to laugh at him. It took nothing from who he was; yet broadened him as a gentleman, an actor, and a respected human being. His; was a rare quality!

His internal mirror gave him room to be class personified; yet beloved actor, that made us laugh in his handsomeness. So many of us can't

MY NAME IS LOVE

be both. We don't know how to be. He did it with ease, and it didn't detract one iota from the respect and admiration we had for him. As a matter of fact, it only endeared us to him. It made us see how one who was at the pinnacle of his profession, and a standard of class; didn't take himself too seriously… To also make us laugh! Somehow, this brought him on our level; where we could touch him with our lives.

Seeing this, allowed me to translate how many of us are in life and relationships. We see ourselves one way. The internal mirror of our heart is small and linear, rather than large and encompassing. This gives us little room to see ourselves as anything, or anyone else. And when others notice the cracks in our armor; we lash out! Rather than look deeper within.

Our perspectives are narrow! We see ourselves, our lives and our world; as leading actors, never in need of an acting coach or further education. The skilled continues practicing his craft lifelong. As a physician practices medicine; never fully mastering. He leaves room for growth through constructive and even destructive criticism. Each instance, he returns to his internal mirror; wide and broad, noticing the chinks in his armor he must repair.

The over sensitive, over confident, self promoting; never find this place and time within. They medicate with the balm of vanity, rather than introspective healing and reconditioning.

We often find such a one argumentative, loud, reclusive or evasive. The outlook from their portal… The problem is the world; not me!

But change we all must do. Dust off and enlarge the internal mirrors of our hearts and minds to reflect our image… Ever expansive, large; and in constant need of tuning.

TOOLS THROUGH THE WISDOM OF GOD

These are the beautiful ones, with a healthy sense of self; never deprecating, but knowing in life, all things must change! Even us, the best and the worst of us; must ever evolve, and succumb to the criticism of our hearts and others. For only in this we learn, we grow; we expand our depth and range in life to become illuminating to others.

We must accept the words of others; the darts and the flares, and find if there be any truth within. For even the darts and the arrows with flames bring light to shine on our internal mirrors; to find us lacking and incomplete.

Only the wise finds reward in this; as a man who finds great treasure. For he can see what may have been sent to hurt, harm or injure… Actually gave him light and space to adjust and enlarge the internal mirror of his heart; producing character. This did not quench his light within; yet only broadened it… To make him more illuminating, and attractive to others; to see!

> ~ PLEASE, PLEASE, PLEASE! ALL COUPLES THAT ARGUE, FIGHT AND DISAGREE… PLEASE USE THIS WISDOM GOD HAS PROVIDED THROUGH THIS AGREEMENT. IT COULD SAVE YOUR MARRIAGE! ~

~ THE AGREEMENT OF DE-ESCALATION! ~

One of the most dangerous places we go in marriage… Is the place of arguments and fighting. It's the most frequent device the enemy uses to reap havoc, cause chaos and destroy our relationships.

There must be an off ramp; to de-escalate from fights and arguments to place us back on our road to peace and purpose. We must heal! We must recover from the wounds and arrows we threw. We must reunite peacefully; apologize and forgive. We must make up and reconnect, so we no longer see each other as enemies, but as teammates and partners in the purpose of God. We mustn't allow the enemy to divide us, separate us, and attempt to move us away from our paths ordained by God!

There must be a signal; a sign, or something that we can use to break the silence, the tension, the distraction… And assist us back to friendship and harmony.

This something… Must be talked about, and mutually agreed upon; well before our explosions. We can't wait until we're angry to put something reasonable in place. This, we must do while there is peace. We must know that life doesn't always move in a straight line. Sometimes we come upon curves of confusion. Things happen! We make mistakes.

The wise couple knows such things will come, and are prepared for them through a contingency plan… A simple or detailed plan to Respond to the situation; rather than Reacting to it.

This will be discussed, and mutually agreed upon; that this will be our behavior in our arguments and disagreements. This will be our exit ramp; to put us back on our freeway to love.

We do harm and damage when we react, rather than respond. A Response is a more controlled reciprocation to a situation or event; that's thought about first before it's release. When we react, we say the first thing that comes out of our mouths; usually unfiltered!

These things hurt; and can do tremendous damage. If not dealt with properly, we can wound someone for years. These hurts will resurface and rear their heads at the most in-opportune times. Especially during arguments! We must apologize and forgive as needed.

We can't continue to walk in our destructive ways. We can't continue to say just anything to each other; just because we're angry or hurt. The

TOOLS THROUGH THE WISDOM OF GOD

Bible warns us of the damage we do with our words. It tells us to "Let no corrupt talk come out of your mouths, but only such as is good for building up, (or edifying)." Ephesians 4:29 It also tells us "A brother who has been insulted (or offended), is harder to win back than a walled city." Proverbs 18:19

As Christian's, we must learn to govern our mouths. Sometimes we look no different from those in the world in arguments and disagreements. And we say we have Christ in our lives and are filled with the Holy Spirit!

None of us are perfect, and we all slip at times; but this shouldn't be our regular behaviors and reactions. How can those that don't know Christ desire Him if We have no restraint or command of our mouths. They'll look at us as hypocrites, who have no more control over our lives than they do. Christ should be evident in our lives.

If we can't govern our mouths and tempers, we should seek help from God. If we can't remain calm through arguments and disagreements; if we lack self control more often than restraint... We need help from God.

Have you ever wondered why God hasn't helped you with your mouth and temper so far? Its because God won't force Himself, or even His help upon us. We must submit to His help by asking for it. The Bible says... "We have not because we ask not." James 4:2

If we thought we were fine like we are because God hasn't changed us in this area of our lives... We fooled ourselves! Today we learned that God hasn't liked our ways at all. He sent His word to illuminate our behaviors, and to ask Him both for forgiveness and for help. This leads us to freedom from ourselves, and our destructive ways.

These ways and behaviors don't automatically go away when we become saved either. They'll stay as toxicity and venom until we confess to God that we have a problem, and need His help.

If you've been hurt, been in a bad relationship... You qualify, and are probably exhibiting these characteristics in your marriage. What's really sad is; when we exhibit these ways before our children. We're poor examples to them for this. We're accountable for teaching them correctly.

My grandparents were married for over 50 years. They were both Christian's who loved the Lord with all of their hearts. I'm sure they had arguments and disagreements, but not once did any of us hear them. And they slept with the door open! We still never heard them arguing. Some of us even slept with them.

They never argued in front of us. We never heard them disrespect each other either. Were they perfect! No! They decided they were going to follow Christ, and weren't going to be bad examples before us!

TOOLS THROUGH THE WISDOM OF GOD

There are two words we must always keep readily in our mouths in marriage... 'I'm sorry!' This is the first step to reconciliation. If you don't apologize... The fences get higher! Barriers get thicker and wider.

Through our pride, we allow our thoughts to carry us away to places they shouldn't go. These corrupt thoughts can influence our behaviors; and we can walk out of the ways of love which are patient, kind, and persevering.

Look at all the critical time we lose due to arguments and not talking. We as a couple; must promise to make this Agreement to De-escalate. Even if we have to write it down and both sign it. Bring it out, and display it where we can see it... To remind us to get back on track to the ways of God, for our marriage and purpose.

Whatever it is, we must mutually decide it together. That Peace Pipe; that places us back on track. On track from looking ugly at each other. From sleeping in the dog house, or our toes at the furtherest edge of the bed; barely holding on to keep us from falling off.

We must have a way to make up. A way to see the larger picture. A way to come back to love and harmony. We must not give room to the enemy through our anger. We must not attempt to hurt one another; with the venom we can spew out of our mouths.

Fences get lowered and removed in a safe and loving environment. They get removed when we lower our voices; and our attitudes line up with the ways of Christ. Saying we're a Christian isn't just when things are going well. This is the difference between us and the world... We carry Christ into all of our situations. This is the difference maker in our lives which shines as light to the unbeliever.

We don't take off Christ and lay down our Christianity when we argue and disagree. Having Christ in our lives is what makes us special and unique in our lives and our situations.

MY NAME IS LOVE

We must take a stand in our marriages! We must confess that we will not allow the enemy to destroy what God has given us.

The purpose of God is upon each one of our marriages. We must keep our hearts pure; lest we be distracted.

We must learn to set aside our pride and govern our mouths. We must lower and remove our fences. We must move ourselves to rejoin in love.

There is a mountain close to where I live that's so steep, trucks can only travel down it at 10 mph. Every so many feet, they must pull off the road and check their brakes to make sure they're not too hot. Two places down the mountain, there are off ramps covered in deep gravel… In case a truck loses it brakes; to save the driver's life.

At the bottom of the mountain, there are over 20 crosses on the wall. These crosses represent all of the truck drivers who have lost their lives due to loosing their brakes coming off that mountain.

How many marriage crosses would be on that wall because the brakes got too hot and we lost our tempers, our composures; control of our mouths and bodies. None of those marriages made it to the off ramp to de-escalate, and to calm down to safety and normalcy. They died! Two people, and the lives of the children; damaged due to pride and selfishness. This is not the will of God for our marriages!

We must remain, realign, rejoin, refocus; renew our walks in Christ through our confessions for help. It's not always the person we blame that's the cause of the problem. We too must search our own hearts and look within our own mirrors. None of us are perfect, so none of us are exempt from this word God; not I, have given!

We must learn to humble ourselves in our anger! Ask for help!

Walk on the side of Christ… Especially when we argue!

"My goodness TJ, I wish I could of heard of this years ago when I was that woman. Truth be told, it's good to hear now because it's easy to lapse into the old me. That's what I knew growing up. I have to ask God for help submitting to the Holy Spirit for guidance, wisdom, restraint, and love.

Thanks again!!"
Debra D'Attoma

LOVE REQUIRES AN ANSWER

The Bible gives us the description of love in 1 Corinthians 13… "Love is patient, love is kind. It does not envy, it does not boast, it is not proud. It does not dishonor others, it is not self-seeking, it is not easily angered, it keeps no record of wrongs. Love does not delight in evil but rejoices

MY NAME IS LOVE

with the truth. It always protects, always trusts, always hopes, always perseveres."

Before we make a mess of our lives and others, we need to consider some prerequisites before we enter a serious relationship.

We must not only ask ourselves if we are capable of meeting these requirements of love for someone. We must also ask... Do we meet their requirements for them loving us! We must also ask... Can they love us? Are they both capable, and willing to love us?

These are very important questions to ask; because some of us have been damaged from previous relationships. If we're not careful, they can leave us hard, cold, callous and emotionally absent.

If we fall into this category, we must acknowledge it, and deal with it... Before we ruin another life, or our own even further.

To know if we're ready or qualified for any relationship, we must ask ourselves if we can meet the requirements of 1 Corinthians 13.

It serves as our yardstick for love; or the absence of it.

TWO DEATHS IN MARRIAGE

God intended there to be two deaths in a marriage. One at the beginning with the couple, and one at the end; when one of them transitions from this life into the next.

Couples must agree before the marriage to die to themselves. A dead man has not needs. He is selfless. He is not sensitive to barbs and arrows. He feels no pain.

TOOLS THROUGH THE WISDOM OF GOD

This doesn't quite describe us amongst the living. But it does give us some good illustrations as to how we can be in any given situation. One of the main reasons we fail in marriages and in relationships; is the very thing that led us there in the first place… Our feelings!

This does more damage than anything. Our eyes wander when we feel greed, and non contentment; with what was given to us. Anger arouses our feelings. We lash out, and seek to hurt others because our feelings were hurt. If we were dead; we wouldn't be subject to such things.

It's not a physical death that we're talking about. It's a Death to Self! Unless both agree before the wedding to subject themselves to this death; we're asking for trouble. It won't work either if only one dies!

That's unfair… And the one living will make life a nightmare for the one that kept their promise to die!

A PRIVILEGE

It's a privilege to be a man. It's an honor to be a husband. It's a blessing to be married. The Bible says… "He who finds a wife finds a good thing and obtains favor from the Lord." Proverbs 18:22

Marriage shouldn't be your chore, nor your burden. Marriage isn't a right; it's a privilege! None of us were forced into marriage. We entered into the institution of marriage on our own accord. We agreed to receive all the rights and privileges of this institution. What we were never told was; there were two things we entered… The marriage and the relationship. The marriage was the easy part. What we are left with to uphold and to honor; is the Relationship!

This is where we meet, relate, commune, communicate, plan, manage, facilitate and work together as one unit called the family. We entered into the institution of marriage, but what awaits us once we enter… Is the Relationship!

This relationship is not self sustaining by any means. It must be nurtured, cherished, fertilized, tended to, appreciated, taken care of, watered; and given to God for reason, direction and purpose.

What it took to get that wife; that husband, will require that and more to keep them. The relationship requires work, effort, commitment, time, energy, dedication, dependability, responsibility, reliability, ingenuity, creativity, giving; and most of all selflessness. Maybe these were things you were never told before you entered into marriage. But now you know; and what you know, you will also be accountable for unto God.

God shares His wisdom to enlighten us, to correct us and to turn us towards our proper paths. Of course, these are things I didn't know before I got married. But I've heard them as God spoke them to my heart… To write them as His scribe.

This I do know… I will walk in ignorance no longer!

LOVE MORE THAN FEELINGS

All of our lives we've associated love with feelings; with emotions, with caring. That's what we've been taught. That's only a part of love. There's another part of love that's required; especially when we enter marriage.

The Bible defines love for us in Corinthians. In its description, it doesn't aline with our usual version of love. I think we've made up our own definition of love; which is lacking, inadequate and misleading. Anytime we attempt to change the precepts of God, we fail; and fall further from the truth. We move further away from morality and what's right in the world.

TOOLS THROUGH THE WISDOM OF GOD

We can look at the world today and see that we've strayed from God's true definition of love. We must move back to realign ourselves with God's true definition of love rather than the watered down version we've conjured up on our own.

This is God's definition of love. It's the only definition of love. Anything that doesn't fall within these parameters; doesn't align with love.

These are God's requirements for love… "Love is patient, love is kind. It does not envy, it does not boast, it is not proud. It does not dishonor others, it is not self-seeking, it is not easily angered, it keeps no record of wrongs. Love does not delight in evil but rejoices with the truth. It always protects, always trusts, always hopes, always perseveres. Love never fails!" 1 Corinthians 13:4-8

Within that entire description of love, I never saw anything mentioned about feelings. There were no goose bumps, butterflies, clouds in the sky; nor any rainbows. The definition mentioned nothing of happiness, elation, rapid heartbeats, sweaty palms, nervousness; or any such thing.

I saw nothing about feelings at all! And this is our primary definition of love! One of us is off base; off kilter in the truth of the precepts of love. God is the one that defined and originated love. Therefore, its up to us to line up with His requirements to experience, and truly say that we love.

Every requirement in God's definition of love requires us to do something, or be something! It had nothing to do with romance, flowers, date nights, kisses or hugs. I saw none of that in there. Although those can be residuals of love.

Love is both energy and effort. Love is discipline, restraint and self control. Love is commitment, dedication, responsibility, reliability and dependability. Love is acts, and behaviors; which demonstrate our

MY NAME IS LOVE

connection towards the good and well being of another. Love seeks to protect, to honor; to respect. Love edifies! It builds! It never tears down or demolishes. It inspires and encourages!

The safety of love releases feelings. This is what we're most familiar with. We've based our entire definition of love on the feelings we obtain and release. We've based love on emptiness; rather than on Acts, through Demonstration.

We've loved for looks; for money, for shallowness. Then we've wondered why our marriage didn't last… Not realizing that feelings only carry us to a certain point. Our feelings can decline over time, and can go up and down. They can't be counted on, nor be depended upon for something as important as love. Love can't hinge upon our feelings.

We must be prepared to love; to be, to do, to perform the acts and behaviors, before we covenant our lives before God with someone in marriage. We can't enter based on our feelings alone; but on our understanding of the precepts of God's definition of love.

We must meet God's requirements for love by being some things, and not being others. God's word says we must be… "Patient, kind, selfless, rejoice with truth, hope, trust and persevere."

Love requires us not to do these things… "Not be boastful, not be selfish, don't keep records of wrong, don't be easily angered, don't be full of pride, and don't delight in evil."

To do better in life, we must align ourselves with the truth. To do better in our marriages, we must align ourselves with God's true definition of love… Love based on acts and behaviors. Not solely based on our unreliable, and non dependable feelings; as we have always done.

We've been deceived about the truth of love!

TOOLS THROUGH THE WISDOM OF GOD

If we say we love; we must be prepared to evaluate the scripture concerning love… To see if we are willing to meet love's requirements. We must demonstrate this through our dedication, and the ability to remain in place of our commitments.

This is how God loves us without condition… He doesn't love us based on His feelings for us. He loves us based on the character of who He is!

DON'T SUBMIT TO ME… SUBMIT TO GOD

Your submission to me will be a chore! You may find it hard to do, even if I'm not a difficult man. It has little or nothing to do with me. It's you! It's your unwillingness. You use me as a crutch; an excuse to not do what God; not I, have required of you.

You'll make every reason why you won't, or you can't. 'You came home late!' 'You didn't take out the trash!' Anything will do!

The truth has always been, your submission isn't unto me. Your submission has always been unto God. You and I both benefit from Our submission to Him. Submitting to God makes it easy to submit; both husband and wives, in our marriage to each other.

The world and many Christian's find this foolish and unnecessary. Christian's should know the requirements of God in marriage before we enter. If we can't fulfill them, then marriage isn't for us. We don't enter to break the rules; living any way we please. Marriage is not an 'Any way we please' type of institution! Nothing about God is. With any Institution; we abide by the rules of entry.

God is a god of Order. He has ordained order in all things; including our marriages. The opposite of order is chaos! It's why our marriages look like we play by our rules; instead of God's.

MY NAME IS LOVE

Submitting our hearts and lives to God; takes the chore out of the work of love.

A TRANSFERENCE

Violence is the Transference of fear from one person to another.

Arguing is the loss of Balance in one person to another.

Encouragement is the transference of Strength from one person to another.

Laughter is the transference of Joy from one to another.

Love is the transference of Light from one person to another.

Passion is the transference of Energy to a person, thing or event.

Humility is the transference of one's unselfish essence unto another.

Unity is the transference of Peace from one person, people; nation to another.

To Uplift is the transference of Power from one person to another.

Restoration is the transference of healing in a body, mind or society.

Education is the transference of Intelligence installed from one person to another.

Hate is the transference of Darkness from one person to another.

TOOLS THROUGH THE WISDOM OF GOD

If we look at each of these things, we can find ourselves in most of them. Some good; some bad. We should strive for the good and take time to study the bad and ask ourselves… How can we correct these things!

Sometimes awareness is the very key to understanding. Sometimes the lack of seeing ourselves, and the lack of the ability to define our situations, leaves us blind and unaware; doomed to repeat our shortcomings.

Label them! Identify them! Become aware of them before you succumb to them. If we know that fighting isn't strength, but weakness leaving us; it tells us how we are beforehand and serves as a stop sign for us to make adjustments.

If we know that arguing and hollering is a state in which we've become unbalanced from our senses of calm, reasoning; of our emotions and control of them, then wisdom intervenes to reset us.

If we know that darkness clouds our hearts to venture into hate. The first question we must ask ourselves is why! Why do we hate? Most times we don't even know why. Oftentimes, there's no good reason. Sometimes it's just not knowing why. Sometimes it's due to hurt. The remedy for hurt is forgiveness. Such things can be remedied with a change of mind and decision; which will lead to a change in heart.

In the situations in our lives; in our interactions with others, there are transferences. Now that we're aware of this, we can be aware of the deposits we make, leave and withdraw in others. The good we strive for. The others, we now have a stop sign called wisdom; to take us on a different path.

Wisdom is the light which enlightens our paths. Now that we know, we can adjust ourselves towards good.

Chapter 8

GOD'S WOMAN

~ Give me what I lack in love for her Lord. To show it. To display it. To live it. To be it for her; that she knows what's real, true and genuine. ~

These words I received from God on 11/19/13...

SHOW THE WORLD HOW TO TREAT A WOMAN. NOTHING LESS THAN A GIFT FROM ME... NOTHING LESS!

IT'S WITHIN MY HEART TO BE

It's within my heart to be... Loving, kind; a gentleman. To know that look of a woman. That one where you see the reflection of love in her eyes towards you. That way she touches you, holds you within her embrace. The curve of her smile in your presence.

Dependable, reliable, trustworthy are her stalwarts. The comfort of her breast; to ease the stress of life. The gentle touch of her hand upon you; as silent as a whisper.

My heart longs for her. At night while I sleep; it never rest. Looking; searching; to the interruption of my sleep. I awake; asking for her presence.

To have that look of love upon me. That look of respect, admiration; appreciation for my life, my purpose... For me. To stand beside me. To walk beside me jointly, in love and united. To allow me to be seen as a light of God in others... Pointing them to purpose and His Kingdom.

To share, to caress, to soothe; life upon all aspects... Spiritually, Physically and Emotionally. To give without measure the abundance of our hearts, neither with fear or apprehension. To know the depths of love, and to explore them as merchants finding treasure. To walk securely and knowingly; the backing, the trust; the devotion of one whose heart's intertwined with mine in love and in life... Jointly together.

My subconscious never sleeps. In my slumber, it searches. I awake longing and exhausted; of its search. I awaken, greeted with the thoughts of my heart; deep and ever flowing.

To know the warmth of her presence. To be seen within her eyes. To know the safety in her smile. The security of her heart; as a vault containing vast riches. A treasure indeed!

I gravitate towards the light... For it's within my heart to be!

Both measuring stick and rod, these words search and define the desires of my heart made light. Who am I; to debate the mandates of my heart... When I have placed them within the privy of God.

BEAUTIFUL...

I made love to you in the deepest of ways... Through closeness, through laughter and through allowing you to see parts of me you've never seen before. Through the simplicity of a dance.

It only showed what we could have. Who we could be together. The brightness of our union could be illuminating in the love and purpose of God assigned.

Beauty has defined itself to me through the experience of you. I'm so grateful for its privilege!

THE CRY

I hear the cry from women… Are there any decedent men left? Your cry is worthy. There's much foolishness in the world today. Deceit is prevalent more than ever in relationships. There's a hidden agenda. Lies are a common thing in a conversation. It's the way of the world.

As a result of such a status, many have been hurt, used, broken, damaged, and some destroyed. Relationships or shall I say, bad relationships; are the quickest way to a broken heart. We all want to be loved. We all want to be cared for. We find these things in a relationship. We were designed to want to receive love and to express love. This is done through relationships. This is also done through our hearts, which is also the most vulnerable parts of us.

To expose our hearts, is to expose the essence of our beings. It's where we live and breathe. It's our core, and the essential part of our feelings, emotions and love. Such a place should not be exposed and open to games, foolishness and wrong individuals. It's one of the most critical decisions we make in life… Who enters this special place which affects all that we are?

Who is special enough to pass through these golden gates which protects our heart, our emotions and feelings? Who is protector, champion, shepherd and farmer; to nourish and care for such valuable and important elements in our lives? The answer is… Not just anyone!

GOD'S WOMAN

Ladies, I know many of you have given up hope in believing there are good and decent men still out there. How do I know? I hear it from God in the words He speaks to me, and I hear it from so many women I share the writings God gives me with. The search is on! It's not a search for a man. There's plenty of men out there. What you want is a good man.

Ladies, this can be both your obligation and the man's. The first thing is your decision making. You must equip yourself with the wisdom of God. Does this man love God and demonstrate his love for Him? Notice I didn't ask, 'Was he a Christian!' We all know that means little these days. People's words mean nothing to God. It's their actions He's concerned about.

God isn't concerned about people's titles either, if you want to know the truth about it. Those titles we throw upon ourselves mean nothing to God. God is always interested in people's lives and results! Being a minister, pastor, bishop or whatever doesn't make us right before God. So ladies, you must know this too when a man approaches you and tries to flatter and impress you with his title or position. Look for humility and service in his life. This will tell you where he stands with God. Arrogance and pride will also tell you where he stands with God.

Again ladies, the bad man isn't for you! You have no business asking God to send you a man and being attracted to the thug, the pimp, the playa, the balla and the whatever. If you're attracted to a man like this, ask God to deliver you from that deceit, and to give you wisdom and awareness to see through that. If you don't, you'll be in a bad, unequally yoked relationship where you'll end up back on your knees asking God to set you free from such a relationship. Wisdom doesn't enter where it doesn't belong!

Ladies, there are men out there; good men who want to do right by one woman. There are men who want to love only you, care for you,

MY NAME IS LOVE

cherish you, and tell the world how proud he is to have you. There is such a man that isn't interested in gamin and playin. A man who just wants one woman to call his own, to settle down with, and be obedient to God for the two of you.

There's such a man who wants to lead his family as God leads him. One who will work and take his place at the head of the household as God has ordained in love, wisdom and humility. Such a man who's willing to be faithful to his wife and his children. One who'll stay in his God ordained place, as a man designed of God.

Ladies, there is such a man out there. I've seen them. I know them. I hear their cry also; pleading for a good woman who will not take their strength and kindness as weakness. The world's got it backwards. The world displays the bad guy as having it together. It's wrong! Running from responsibilities and commitments are never a sign of strength and doing what's right. These men are out there and they're looking for you. But you first have to wake up, take your eyes off of the bad guy, who'll ruin you.

Ask God to deliver you from that attraction. Ask Him to give you the wisdom to be attracted to the good man He has for you. It's only then you'll walk in and fulfill your purpose in life, by partnering with a man who you'll help to complete the destiny God assigned the two of you to build His kingdom on earth.

Ladies, this is a serious decision! Besides your salvation, it's one of the most important decisions you'll make in your life.

You'll need to use this wisdom God provided to make it correctly!

GOD›S WOMAN

TRUST ACCOUNT

A woman isn't given... She is won! A woman doesn't give herself to a man willingly. A man has to win her over to his side called a relationship. One of the most important requirements of a woman's release of herself... Is Trust!

A woman is an accountant. She is CEO of The Bank of Trust. Within this bank, deposits and withdrawals are made. There are no loans here! Nothing is borrowed. She lends nothing! She has no free calendars. Nothing is taken out and brought back. This is not a car dealership. There are no free test rides!

For in times past... Others have given away for free, what should have only be paid with the currency of Commitment and Sacrifice! This woman knows this; and conducts her life accordingly.

This is a special bank in which trust is deposited or withdrawn only. She stands over every transaction, and carefully weighs it as her vault contains the greatest treasure on Earth... Her Heart!

So now we see why God has shown us that a woman isn't given; she's won. A woman doesn't give such a valuable item away. It's won over with trust, dependability, reliability and commitment. Only then is it delicately released within the hands of a man. Hands of a man neither soiled nor slippery; but steady, strong and able to contain such wealth.

A woman monitors the ways of a man; watching and weighing his every transaction. Through truth, kindness and awareness; he makes deposits into his account. Through lies, foolishness and games; he makes withdrawals.

At times he even overdraws his account, and is released; and told he no longer qualifies for the treasures her vault contains.

MY NAME IS LOVE

Because she's wise, she's aware of counterfeits. She's aware of those who say they're making deposits, but are only playing with Monopoly money. They're quickly shown the exit door.

Some are slick. Some come with money that looks real; yet it's fake. For this, she had to examine it more closely. God has given her discernment to know the wolves disguised as sheep. They talk of making lofty deposits with false tender. They too are shown the exit!

Then there is one who makes little, yet consistent deposits into her bank. His money is real. His goal; his intentions are to one day be rich with the world's most greatest treasure.

He's focused. He's determined. He regularly makes deposits of kindness. He adds to his account the currency of gentleness. He comes with the notes of awareness and tremendous concern for her, and what's guarded behind the security of those walls. One day he wants to make enough deposits within her bank to open its doors.

So he comes daily even with change, to make small deposits. All are not large. He's not rich; he's consistent. He knows little things add up, and gradually fills up an account. All deposits count, and he's not making any major or substantial withdrawals either. He's not perfect. He never intends to make withdrawals, but at times life has taxed him, he forgot to do something; or he was human and just slipped.

The times he does, he fills out an application and submits a Form of Apology. He's not ashamed. He wasn't too proud to let others see him making this apology deposit. He left his pride outside of this precious institution. This man is looking for treasure; more precious than gold.

One day, after he has made many deposits; large and small… Minimal and minor, through care, reliability, truth and consistency. She opens her vault and releases her heart to him. He has neither tricked, fooled or deceived his way here. He has come as a man seeking what's valued more on Earth than anything.

The Heart of a Woman!

A GOOD WOMAN

What a good woman does to a man… She causes him to take a look at his armor. He realizes he has some chinks in it. It makes him stand up straight and tall, and to get busy buffing out those chinks in his armor. He no longer wants them, for he wants to shine. He may not have known he had them, until she appeared. She illuminated parts of his life that would increase him, and make him better.

Oh the woman that carries the wisdom of God; that knows how to use her gifts to influence, to persuade; to motivate a man. She uses the softness of her voice, and the kindness of her ways to edify. She builds with her words, and he responds. She makes him believe he can do anything! It's her gift from God as a multiplier. She magnifies his potential, and nurtures his faults. She's both.

She makes him realize why he's alive. She pushes him to discovery, and propels him to greatness. Through God; she's the X factor in his life. He wants to examine himself. He wants what's best for him and others. Now he's alive! He discovers… He merely existed before!

She makes him soar; reaching the stars and beyond. Her belief in him, causes great belief in himself. What was dormant, she has brought alive. What was hidden, she shines her light upon.

She was created for greatness; to enlighten and illuminate. A good woman in his life!

THE MANIFESTATION OF MY HEART

She will come to me, the woman I've always wanted and desired; beautiful inside and out. No more fighting, no more fussing; arguing... .Peace, Love & Joy! She will walk past many to come to me; just for me. She is mine. I am hers. We are each other's!

Beauty with tremendous substance. Absolutely beautiful; yet so down to Earth. Loving, gentle, sweet, giving, kind towards me and others with a heart of gold. She will come to me; be drawn to me in life, love and the purpose of God upon my life.

She will be by my side, stay by my side always; in all things. So much love, joy, partnership, compassion, companionship, passion, depth; romance. She will love me as I've always wanted and needed to be loved.

She will be so close to me; my very best friend and lover. Holding hands, laying on laps, picnics in the living room, making love anywhere in the house, giving herself, her body, mind and soul; everything to me completely without restraint or chore.

These are... The manifestations of my heart!

YOU CAN'T BABYSIT A MAN... YOU CAN MULTIPLY HIM

Society today has been flipped; turned around and backwards. Where is the man and woman of yesterday, who took pride in themselves and everything they touched. What about your word being your bond; integrity and such things. Where's the gentleman that holds the door for a lady, pushes out her chair for her at the table; and remains standing until she's seated. What happened to basic manners and common respect for people; for each other. Because the times have changed;

doesn't mean that we should change with it, in its most opposite directions.

Where are morals and standards these days. What about standing for something good and right. To see a gentleman with class, dignity and refined; I have to look at an old Cary Grant movie for my example.

Men are different today. It's as if we don't know who we are. We've been told so many things; yet we've lacked those basic things which define us. Those basic fortitudes, that are unshakable no matter who tries to tell us something, or make us different.

The bar was set high for men in the generation of my grandfather. These men worked. They married. They stayed married. They took care of their families. They dressed nice and presentable wherever they went. They raised their children with morals, values and standards. They didn't just tell them these things; they modeled them before them everyday.

Were they perfect! No! But they kept the bar high that their generations before them raised. They kept that bar; that standard of conduct and excellence raised high, and they never let it fall an inch.

This is not us today! Not even close! But this is who we must strive to become again; through awareness, education and example. I've never noticed until now that the word example is prefaced with the word 'Exam'. It means that we must pass our exams of life to become Examples to others!

A woman can't babysit a man; she can only multiply him. She's a multiplier. Whatever you give her she multiplies. But a man must give a woman something to multiply. She's not a fixer or a restorer from nothing. No! She multiplies the potential given to her, and increases who a man already is.

I was shown from the generations of my grandfather; if you want a woman... First get you a job! Have yourself a car. Get you a home! Living with your parents is a deal breaker! Have some plans, some goals in life. Then when you have filled those squares; send for the woman you plan to marry and settle down with. That's what I was shown, and I paid attention. These were the SOP's (Standard Operating Procedures) for manhood.

A woman can't babysit a man not working, who has no potential, no drive, no ambition. A man playing video games; living at home with his mom. A woman multiplies what a man already has. She doesn't make him a man... She makes him a better man!

But a woman today must use wisdom, and now awareness to know she's not a fixer; she's a multiplier! She must chose a man that comes to her already with maturity and substance. She can't place those things there. She'll wear herself out, and ruin herself for the good man she's destined to receive.

Now that we know, we must do better, we must be better... We must chose better for us and our futures.

WHEN I WANNA KNOW

(Excuse my abuse of 'Want to.' It's just my deeper expression)

When I wanna know love, it's your example I see. It's your image impressed upon my mind.

When I wanna be held, it's your arms I see around me. It's your presence pressed close against me.

When I wanna know companionship, I remember your ways and our times together.

When I wanna look into the soul of another, it's within your eyes I begin my search.

When I long for you... It's time, space and distance I must diminish.

When I thought I could get no closer to you, I found more area, space and depth; in which to venture.

I find these things within you. You are these, and so much more.

You are Inexhaustible to me!

I wanna know. I wanna know more!

SEND ME A MULTIPLIER

You give her looks, she multiplies it into beauty. You gave her substance, she has turned it into character and charm. You give her grace, she's a joy and a delight.

You sent her to me, she's now a companion. My partner in life. You saw I was lonely. She now occupies space, time and togetherness with me. You saw I needed help, she brought with her efficiency and care.

Whatever you give her... She Multiplies!

She multiplies good, and calls it living. She multiplies time, and makes them memories. She multiplies space, and calls it togetherness. She multiplies togetherness, and makes it romance.

She ushers in the Sun. She quiets the moon to sleep. She brightens the new day with her presence. She's a joy to behold.

MY NAME IS LOVE

How I've longed for her. How I've desired her with the very soul within me. My subconscious has cried out for her. Please come to me!

We have found each other! As it was always meant to be.

You have given her charm, beauty and grace. You've shared with her Your very Essence. She's multiplied it... Into a Woman!

BEAUTY TO BEAUTY

That way she looks into your eyes. That look that passes as light to soul. That look of admiration, respect and desire all into one. For one... You!

It seldom finds its equal in life. It's love, it's honor. It's saying I believe in you; in the love, in the environment that you shelter me within.

Hold me close my dear, and let me feel the brilliance of God next to me. Lavish me in the love that only He can give.

Let me feel His heart beat through yours; to mine. Let me embrace the majesty of His kindness wrapped in human life beside me.

Oh Great and Wonderful; thank You for who and what You've given. Some will never know the bounty; the joy!

Few; and I, have Your wonders seen and embraced in delight; through the eyes of another. Through one so lovely and kind.

Thank You Majesty, for the privilege, the honor; to behold the joy of a woman. Wrapped in humanity... Wrapped in love!

GOD'S WOMAN

BEAUTY REDEFINED

The softness of her eyes. The kindness she exudes. The gentleness of her words towards me and others. The touch of her hand. Her fingers mingled into mine. The way she shows concern; compassion. The sweetness of her ways. She has redefined beauty to me.

YOUR VOICE IS DEFINING

I once heard a man who fought during wartime say that he was hit so frequently by his enemy, at some point Mother Nature took over, and it didn't matter how hard he was hit; he could no longer feel it.

It's like going up a mountain in a car, at some point something happens within our ears to protect us from the pressure and damage to our ear drums. It's something that happens automatically, without us telling our bodies.

A woman has a special tool given to her by God; but if she's not aware of its value and purpose... She'll misuse it. In her misuse, she can tear down and even destroy. She can reduce something that's seven feet tall down to two inches. She can damage and confuse, something that was meant to be seen with clarity. A woman unaware, or uncaring of this; can ruin her marriage and her home. She can run a man away... With her voice!

The Bible says this... "It is better to live in a corner of the housetop than in a house shared with a quarrelsome wife." Proverbs 21:9 It also says this... "Let a man meet a she-bear robbed of her cubs, rather than a fool in his folly." Proverbs 17:12

Neither one of these we want to face! It's no way to live. It's not how life was intended to be lived. The man who married the woman in Proverbs

MY NAME IS LOVE

31 praised his wife. Her children praised her. Her servants praised her. What made this woman different!

One man is trying to get away from his wife. It appears that he's more content to be in the corner of the rooftop, than to be in her presence. Imagine how he felt when he heard her footsteps coming! Man, he was in for it! Why?

Was she a product of marrying a bad man, or was this her personality that had soured over time due to hurt, pain and bitterness. Was this who she'd become; that her husband now hides from her. Has he become like our hearing in high elevations, our ears become silent to protect our ear drums from bursting! Has he become like that soldier who fought in the war, beaten so badly… That Mother Nature took over to protect his body; so he could no longer feel the beating through shock. Is this how God called us to be in marriage; as husband and wife! A man is to be seen in his home, not hiding in it; trying to escape from his wife.

We as men can be stubborn, hard-headed, and foolish. Somewhere along the way, some of the hurt we face in a woman, came from a previous man or men. Sometimes we're wounded by the collateral damage. Sometimes we're the cause of the hurt and pain in a woman.

Regardless, God didn't create the woman He took time, great attention to detail, placed specific characteristics within her… To be so damaged that what she mostly does is scream and holler. Her voice is a tool; given to her of God. The voice of woman, was given to her by God to amplify; not to tear down.

A woman can reduce her husband to less than who he was intended to be with her words, and the manner in which she speaks them. She can confuse him, and cause him to misinterpret and doubt his worth from God; and the importance of his assignment from Him.

GOD'S WOMAN

Or worse, he can seek to hear kind words and encouragement elsewhere. It's a trick of the enemy if you fall into his trap. His goal... To destroy God's family, the purpose assigned to it, and its assistance in building the Kingdom of God.

Husbands, stop your foolishness! Stop pushing your wife so far with dumbness, that all she knows is to come out swinging with her words. Words that cut like knives, and sting like venom. Words that are intended to belittle your manhood, and decrease your standing in her eyes. All of this is wrong! All of it tares our families apart. The enemy sits back and smiles believing he destroyed each one. He mocks what God has ordained; and we allow him. Both of us; husband and wife.

Husbands, we must be better than to drive our wives to bitterness and a boisterous voice. We must seek to invest into her with love, gentleness, kindness and understanding. We must stop making withdrawals from her. She's a receiver. We must make deposits in the bank of her heart and emotions.

Ladies, maybe your heart has been on overload for too long! Maybe you carried baggage into this marriage, that should have been left on the doorstep of your last relationships. Maybe your husband has been foolish, and uneasy to deal with. Turn him over to God, but don't allow him to ruin your beauty from within. Show him these words God; not I, have given so he's aware of his responsibility to God and to you. Help him to change with the smoothness, kindness and gentleness of your words. Your words carry tremendous power and weight.

Enable him! Don't disable him. Lift him up! Speak to him what you desire him to be; and your words will manifest before your eyes. See him through the eyes of God, and not your own. This will make your journey lighter and easier. Your spoken words will no longer be a chore; but your delight. For you are now as an artist; sculpting the masterpiece you'll make through time and effort.

MY NAME IS LOVE

One day, your husband will thank you. One day, your children will thank you. One day you'll stand before God, and He'll thank you.

Let go of the pain! Let go of the bitterness! Let go of the anger too!

Ladies… regain the gift of your voice, from God!

OUTCRIES OF MY HEART

Father, you have given me such a heart to love. In my sleep, it cries out; reaches. It longs to be touched; caressed and massaged with love.

That one; that physical one that brings Your delights. Your closeness and the privilege of You.

In my state of subconscious; outcries my heart. The longing; it carries over into the dawn. For her. To be near her. To lavish with the abundance, You have deposited within me.

Share my life and dreams; my desires. Come to me in the new day; fresh and new. Distribute your gifts; your bounty into our lives.

Be the light that all can see. The reflection of the Almighty. The salt that seasons, and others thirst for. Come to me; to us, and lavish our love with the brightness of your being.

You're in my dreams; from the abundance of my heart. I desire to meet you in the light… When I rise, and throughout the day.

You bring a part of me that only God can give. I long for His presence in you. The touch; the softness of you; your ways bring delight.

GOD'S WOMAN

I am forever changed because of you. You allow me to be. You enhance all that I am. You inspire all that I need to be. You make me feel alive. You set me on my path to living.

I'm forever grateful for your being. Reliable, responsible, dependable… There!

You change the direction of my wind. You give light to Sun and Moon. You are the compass that points North in my life. Your council; ever in tenderness and love.

To me; you are everything. Sent from Heaven above to assist me on my path and purpose for God in life. We build His Kingdom together; in love and by the light of our example.

Your essence breaths life to me… The outcries of my heart!

UNREACHABLE & UNOBTAINABLE

One of my dear friends said something to me today that was so true. It was something I'd never though about before.

When God gives me writings on women and marriage, most of the time the woman in Proverbs 31 will be used as an example. My friend said something to me today that made sense; probably for a lot of women.

There was a time in her life where she felt like she couldn't measure up to the description of this amazing woman in Proverbs. She felt that her qualities and character were unreachable and unobtainable. After all, you have to look closely for the secret of how this woman became this remarkable wife, mother, businesswoman and administrator of her home and family.

MY NAME IS LOVE

It's only through the wisdom of God showing me; that I knew how she became this woman. The fact is, this woman was more than likely already on her path to becoming this incredible wife, even before she was married. It's not like she just got married one day, and decided to be this person. I believe she knew the secret to being this woman before she was married. It's who she was! Being married only magnified who she was, because she was placed in an environment to succeed.

Why do we get married?

We get married for love, loneliness, companionship, company... To share our lives with someone. We may have our reasons for getting married, but God has His own.

The Bible says... "He who finds a wife, finds a good thing and obtains favor from the Lord." Proverbs 18:22 God's reason for our marriage may differ from ours. God assigns purpose and protection to our marriages.

For each marriage in Christ, there is a purpose assigned. That purpose for all Christian marriages is to be light and salt to the marriages of the world that don't know Christ. If there are children, you're to be the model for the success of their marriages one day in the future.

God also designed the marriage to protect us from the world. Within the marriage, we're free to meet our sexual, emotional and physical needs. We meet our needs for companionship, support, and to walk out the purpose of God assigned to us. All we need, we should find within that marriage.

The woman in Proverbs 31 knew the secret of the success of her marriage before she entered. It wasn't just her relationship with Christ.

Many Christian women today say they have a relationship with Christ, but their marriages look nothing like this! They control, manipulate

GOD'S WOMAN

and dominate their marriages, and mistakenly appoint themselves as leader and head of the household. It's one thing to say we're saved. It's another to say we've submitted our lives to Christ!

At the wedding, she made many promises she didn't plan to keep. She didn't want to be controlled, so she began the process of taking her improper position in the marriage. She did this by lifting herself up; by tearing her husband down.

Her mind works differently than his, so she began to run mental circles around him. She starts 'air arguments;' with him for no reason, to get him off balance. She criticizes him to make him doubt himself, and who he really is. She confuses him, saying he did something he didn't do. She'll almost have him believing he did it too. She manipulates him by withholding what isn't hers to withhold… Her body and sex; to disrupt his ego and his manhood. Did I mention these are Christian wives!

This fight started long ago with the fall of Adam in the garden. Adam and his wife enjoyed perfect harmony in marriage. Part of the punishment from God to all women was, God would now establish an order in the marriage. Before sin, there was no need for this. Sin multiplies. Adam was given one commandment from God. Moses was given ten!

Now, because order had physically been established by God, the Bible says to the married woman… "Thy desire shall be to thy husband, and he shall rule over thee." Genesis 3:16 What this means is that a woman would now desire to rule where she wasn't appointed to rule. She would desire to take the place of the man; but that would be the place God ordained him to be. She would fight him in this, through conflict and turmoil!

So how did the woman in Proverbs 31 overcome this obstacle! How is her story in the Bible as an example to every woman today! What made her so successful. What had her husband being a success in the community and in his career; praising and blessing her! What caused her children, her handmaidens and the people she conducted business with to respect and honor her!

Was she born with special qualities. How was her worth more than rubies! Was she well educated and highly intelligent. Why do women, thousands of years later often feel like they can't measure up to who she was. What made her so unique; so different!

It was simply her Choice! She chose to be this remarkable woman! Her heart, mind and body followed her decision. But the key to her decision was this… "A woman that fears the Lord shall be praised!" Proverbs 31:30

The fear of the Lord; her reverence, respect and obedience, allowed her to be this phenomenal wife, mother and woman. Even before she married, she chose to allow God to be Lord over her life and decisions. Her reverence and obedience to God were like the fragrance placed on the feet of Jesus; although it would be a thousand years before He was born.

What did she derive from her decision to reverence God as her lifestyle? She garnered a peaceful home. A loving, respectful and very appreciative husband. She had respectful children who loved and adored her. She obtained it all, by elevating God as the head of her life.

Her reverence produced excellence in every facet of her life. Ladies, now you know what made her so special. God must take first place in your life. It will quench your desires to go where you don't belong, and shine in the places you were ordained to be.

By the way, my friend who once thought being this kind of wife was unobtainable; she also became like the woman in Proverbs. I asked her how she did it. This is what she told me. "When my husband did something and got on my nerves, I turned him over to God, and let God deal with him!"

She began to praise her husband and he began to do things she needed of him. She no longer lived her life for her husband. What she did, she did unto the Lord! He, and their marriage reaped the benefits. It was no longer about him. It was no longer a chore. It was about how she desired to please God.

The thing we least understand is, the ways of God are different than the ways we think. To live we must die! To gain we must let go of! To have we must give! This is the opposite of what we've been taught all of our lives.

It doesn't make sense to our natural minds. This is why we don't do it! It's awkward and unorthodox. It's putting mud on our eyes to receive our sight. It's dipping three times in the dirty Jordan for our healing. These things don't make sense to us. But it makes perfect sense to our spirit man. It's called obedience to God.

We must put aside whether it makes sense or not, and out of faith… Just do it! The spirit part of us must lead us in our decisions. If God has told you to do something that seems foolish… You're lined up for a miracle… If you do it!

What did it do to my friend's marriage? "It set her free," she said! She let go of her life to gain it! She became a woman worth more than rubies… A woman worthy to be praised.

She discovered the secret of the woman in Proverbs. The fear; the reverence of the Lord… Will produce a Woman of Excellence!

MY NAME IS LOVE

I SPEAK TO YOU THROUGH MY TOUCH

My hand, at the small of your back, says your mine; my lady. Not as in possession or ownership… But as in my responsibility; my care for you.

Your fingers intermingled, intertwined within mine, says we're jointly connected as one. The smoothness of my hand against your face, says I cherish and adore you.

The way I touch you; it's all communication. It's my way of speaking to you without words. It's my language of love; my message, my means of affection. Therein; my passion abides for you.

Within my fingers are expression. When I run my hand down your arm, I'm saying to you how much you mean to me; how much I appreciate you. When I rub your feet and legs, I'm saying I understand you; when you're tired and in need of relief through rest. The touch of your hair; to run my fingers through it, says you're so amazing and beautiful to me.

To hold you in my arms, proclaims you mean the world to me. I hold you near me; in that space reserved only for you. You alone receive the nearness of me; and I you.

We are one together in life, love and living. These are the expressions; my language of love to my beloved… Through my touch!

WORDS FOR HER

I've had the privilege of you. I know absolutely and for sure… I never want to be without you!

I miss you so much. My heart aches! I think about you constantly. So I write it down. Maybe I'll share it with you. But for now, it helps me deal with you not being here.

Let me taste the sweetness of your lips. Feel the softness of your skin. Know the smoothness of your shapeliness. I marvel at you. I'm marveled by you. You contain in One, all I ever need. You're my storehouse. You're my haven I run to for rest. Your brightness illuminates me. Your volume amplifies me. I'm better because of you. I'm more as a result of you. My desire is to be more, and do more because of the light you shine upon me.

When you cry, my heart melts. In those moments of sensitivity, I long to be there for you. To comfort you in my arms. Your sensitivity is beautiful to me. In it, I see the softness of your heart. I see the expanse of it, and all the capacity you have to care.

I have not fallen in love with you… .I'm Standing; and will always continue to Stand in Love with You. Which means I'm totally aware of my senses… I'm in control of my choices. It means I see with clarity who and what stands before me… My gift from God; my very own rib, surgically and strategically taken from me, and given back to me in the form, shape and amazement of your being.

Only God could give me such insight; illuminate my mind with such truth, and desire only to please you with a pure motive and intention. Only God… And I'm humbled in His giving!

WOMEN YOU SHAPE THE WORLD

Without women, there would have only been two people that lived on Earth… Adam and Eve. Adam, created from the Earth by God. Eve, created from the rib of Adam. They were the only two humans not born; but created.

Since then, every child, including Jesus; was born of a woman. God tells me something very critical and enlightening about this fact… Women shape the world we live in.

MY NAME IS LOVE

Women, you are the portal to life! Every life comes through a woman. Every human on Earth was the choice of a woman. She's the source of our families which make up society. It's her choice, or her allowance, not man's, that brings forth children. Sure man has a part in it, but it's the woman's decision which allows the creating of a child.

This is a very critical decision to have responsibility for. This decision can't be taken lightly or without thought, planning and the proper environment. Our children are products of her decision.

A man wants; a man desires. But it's the woman who has the decision making capabilities. This is crucial in life and the world.

Today our world is in chaos. Marriages of Christian families and those that are not Christian household are failing. This leaves a deficit in the family, with our children growing up without both parents in their lives.

So many single mothers are raising children without a father around. It's not the plan of God. It's more in line with the plan of the enemy to disrupt and destroy families.

Seeing that the woman bares such a critical role in society, it would only stand to reason the seriousness of her choices and decisions in a man.

Christian and all ladies, the time is gone for you to make poor decisions regarding who you allow in your life. You can no longer afford to be tricked and fooled, then left with a child and the father is no where to be found, or has moved on to the next woman. You are the gatekeeper to life in connection with God; who brings forth the life you carry within.

Ladies, you can no longer afford to be attracted to the bad guy. Yeah he's fine and all that, but you must make long term decisions based on what's right; rather than looks.

GOD›S WOMAN

If a person wasn't right for you in the beginning, they're not going to be right for you and your children later. You can't afford bad in your life; neither can your children.

You must chose a man that's good for you, good to you, and will be a responsible husband for you and your children one day. You can't afford to raise a grown man. You can't afford a man that doesn't work, or doesn't want to work.

You must know the plans and future a man has, because your life will be tied to his. You must know how he is when he's angry. You must know how he manages his money. You must know if he's able, and capable of, providing you with a home and security. You must know how sincere and serious he is about God, or if he doesn't have Christ in his life. You must know this by the fruit he displays in his life; not by his words. A man can tell you anything, but his life has to line up with those words.

Ladies, this is important too… You must stop seeing the good men God sends to you as weak. You're damaged and you've had dysfunction in your life through bad relationships. So you run him off and push him away. You don't recognize the good and decent man God sent to be a blessing in your life.

There's nothing weak about a gentleman. Theres nothing weak about being responsible, reliable and trustworthy. There's nothing weak about a man that wants to marry you, love you and provide a good life for you. There's nothing weak about a man that accepts that he must love you as Christ loves the church, and would be willing to lay down his life for you. That's true strength. That's the kind of strength displayed by Jesus.

The world has got you fooled into believing that a bad man is good for you, and a good man is weak. It's a lie that Satan uses to trick, deceive and fool you; to keep you from living in the fullness of your potential. God has shared this truth with us today… Ladies, you are

MY NAME IS LOVE

the gatekeepers in partnership with God in bringing forth life into the world.

Now that you know this truth, you must adjust your choices and decisions. What you have is priceless! God has given you a critical responsibility in life… Bringing forth children. Ladies, you and the world can no longer afford to fulfill this critical role without wise decisions.

The decision is not the man's… Its yours. You must be wise in your critical decision.

We've allowed the world to tell us what was cool and acceptable, rather than God.

These words were spoken by Jesus… "They are not of the world, even as I am not of the world." John 17:16 They, meaning those who at that time were followers of Christ during His life on Earth. They, meaning us that would become redeemed through His blood by His acceptance after His resurrection.

The point is this… Jesus did not take us out of the physical world when we accepted Him. It's here we would remain. However; our citizenship would change along with our outlook, decisions and our priorities.

We would now be born again; without the formation of a physical birth through our mothers. This re-birthing would be through our Father God, by the way of Jesus.

Although we would remain on Earth after this transition, our citizenship would change. We would now become members of the Kingdom of God. Now being residents of a Heavenly kingdom, our lifestyles would change.

What was old, would now be made new. We would no longer be slaves to sin and foolishness. We would have a new nature; one not of this world. This would bring about a change in our behaviors, our choices; our decisions; and the way we look at life and our lives.

What this would equate to is… We wouldn't be the same people, nor live the same old ways; but differently. Where we were once citizens of the world and blended in; now we've blended out. We've become a peculiar people! We now generate light, and produce salt; to draw and attract others out of the world. We don't do this by being similar; but by being different.

The most important things that must change is our choices and our decisions. We can no longer afford to live the same lives we once did.

Unfortunately, even we as Christians have allowed the world to tell us what we think is cool, rather than God. This has to stop! We're ruining our lives, our families and our reputations as a result of it.

THAT SOMEONE

Someone who will stand beside me in purpose; in delight, without chore. My good, my kindness, my love; will not be taken advantage of, nor taken for granted… But appreciated, respected, reciprocated; admired.

We will be love in delight, with joy and great expression… Giving thanks to God for each other. For chance, opportunity and expression.

Our love; A beauty to behold!

Walk with me. Talk with me. Love with me on many levels. Go with me to places anew and delightful. Our love is ageless, timeless; not subject to wear.

MY NAME IS LOVE

We will walk in full expression of love and freedom; walking in our purpose from God. She'll find great delight in me, and I in her. Together always. A full expression of love, peace, togetherness, partnership, companionship and workers together; building the Kingdom of God.

She is my full expression of beauty, of love; of desire. She gives of herself completely, freely and continuously... In the delight and joy of her creation!

A LESSON FROM A BAD HABIT

I've learned so much from this wonderful woman. She's my big Sis in Christ, and my amazing friend Lucille.

She has an incredible ability to show vulnerability through honesty. In other words, she tells me things without fear of my judgement, seeing her sideways or differently. If anything, it has caused me to endear her even more.

Although we grew up in the same place, neither one of can figure out how our friendship and closeness began or developed. We laugh about it, and just thank God for the privilege!

Lucille tells me things from a woman's perspective. I help her understand things from a man's. We help each other grow in our walks with God.

One day Lucille told me of a time when her husband did something that bothered her. It was just a bad habit he'd probably done before he married her. But it bothered her!

She asked him politely and non offensively, if he would stop this behavior. He apologized, as he just didn't realized it was offensive, and bothered her.

154

GOD›S WOMAN

Here's where the spiritual growth enters the story! Lucille, in her beautiful honesty, told me some incredible things that day.

First she said… "At first I saw it as weakness when he changed his behavior. But God let me know, this is what I asked Him for. I began to love the change in him, and wanted even more!"

When my friend first saw weakness in her husband in his willingness to change his behavior; this can be a very common first response from a woman. The problem is, some women stay there, with their opinions and behaviors towards their husbands. Lucille was wise!

At first, her flesh told her to see him as weak for submitting to her request of him. But her spirit intervened, and told her the truth! Her spirit told her, this is what he was supposed to do. She was supposed to approach her husband in a calm manner and address the issue. She explained what it was, and how it made her feel. They addressed it! He modified his behavior!

The spiritual ramifications came afterwards when she saw his behavior at first as weak. So many women stay in this state. They want changes in their husband, and see him sideways when he modifies his behavior… Instead of being rough, hard, rude; stubborn and unyielding.

Her husband did what every man should have done. Lucille did what every woman should have done. She listened to the wisdom of God within her, to see the spiritual truth of what transpired through the simplicity of a bad habit.

She saw God work through her husband with a modification in his behavior. She then wanted more and more of it. Although her first response to his change was incorrect, she quickly yielded to the truth.

MY NAME IS LOVE

Ladies, don't let your flesh, and the ways of the world, distort the truth of seeing a good man as being weak because he obeys the conviction of God within him. This is the farthest thing from weakness! What you're witnessing is true Strength; personified through a man!

Check yourself! See it right through God's eyes… Not the disillusioned eyes of your flesh!

SAMPLE YOU!

God says some people don't want you, they just want to sample you!

A man walks up to a woman and tells her everything she wants to hear. He tells her how beautiful she is, and how much he's in love with her.

A man will tell a woman anything to get what he wants. It's not what a man says to a woman that really matters… It's what he does for her that shows he really cares for her, or not.

A man who wants something from a woman seeks to impress her with words, because he knows he lacks in deeds. This man uses his words because he's in a hurry. He's in a hurry because he doesn't plan to stay.

His words are shallow. They never point to a future or a commitment. He's not interested in the woman for who she is on the inside… Her dreams, her goals, her desires. He doesn't want to hear those type of things. They're boring and uninteresting to him. He's only interested in the external; physical appearance of a woman. Because he doesn't want her as the complete woman she is. He just wants a part of her.

In other words as God said to me, "He doesn't want you, he just wants to sample you!" And once he's had a sample of you, he loses interest and moves on to the next challenge or buffet on his menu. It's sad, but it's true! I never knew this until God spoke these words of truth to me.

GOD'S WOMAN

Everyday, our young ladies and even married women, fall into this trap; believing the grass is greener on the other side, by falling for flattering lies. Only to find out after they've given up their marriage, family, children, home, security and what God has intended to bless them with. Now they've been robbed; left and abandoned.

They were only A Sample to someone! We must be wiser!

DO WOMEN WANT TO BE

The world is in chaos. We live far from the precepts God established for humanity.

The Bible describes the ideal woman in Proverbs 31 as such… "She is far more precious that rubies. The heart of her husband trusts in her, and he will have no lack of gain.

She does him good, and not harm, all the days of her life. She opens her mouth with wisdom, and the teaching of kindness is on her tongue. Her children rise up and call her blessed; her husband also, and he praises' her. Many women have done excellently, but you surpasses them all. A woman that fears the Lord shall be praised!" Proverbs 31:30

Are there women like this today? Do women strive and desire to have these qualities in their lives? Do they even know the standards of God! Do they know the yardstick to measure where they are, and where God expects them to be? Do they even care?

I'm talking about Christian women! The women in the world aren't concerned with the standards of God. But all of these qualities should be on the radar of every Christian woman; especially if she's married! This is your job performance review.

MY NAME IS LOVE

When I worked, every year my manager had a meeting with me twice a year. The first meeting was to announce my job performance standards. She would go over each one with me, to make sure I understood what was required of me. Each standard was given a rating; below average, average, good or excellent.

Each year, I looked forward to this meeting with my manager. These standards would indicate, based on my performance and factual information, how well I did or didn't do my job. I wanted to know what was expected of me; so I could exceed the standards set for me. At the end of my meeting, I gave my manager my personal plan for my performance appraisal.

The first year I told her I planned on exceeding in 1 out of 4 of my standards, as I was still learning my job. I did! The second year, I told her I planned on exceeding in 4 out of 5 of my standards, in the complications of my job. I did! The third year I expressed to her that I was now a journeyman, and I'd planned on exceeding in all 5 of my standards. Unfortunately, I got injured and my doctors retired me from working.

The point is this… I knew what was expected of me, and I moved towards excellence. With Christ as Lord of my life, I represent Him in all things I do. Whatever I do, the world is a witness; either good or bad. I strive to draw others to Christ by my example. I strive in whatever I do, and all that I am; to walk in Excellence before Him.

It's what the amazing lady that Solomon wrote about in Proverbs… She had those standards. If she was going to be married; she was going to be excellent at it. At some point, she made up her mind to be excellent. God established a desire in her heart. She acknowledged it, accepted it, and moved towards it!

What are our Christian women doing today... Twerking and following the standards of the women of the world! Is being such a woman even a thought in their mind; let alone a goal of pursuit!

Too many find themselves seeking control of their man and marriage, instead of releasing themselves under the guidance of Christ. It's why our Christian marriages look no different from the world's, and our divorce rate is just as high!

The best a woman can be in a home and marriage is an Administrator. She wasn't desired nor ordained by God to be head, or leader. She was created to be partner, and help meet the purpose of God assigned to that family.

We have taken things too far. We have moved miles away from the standards, and order of God for our lives, our homes and our marriages. It's why they're in disarray and confusion. They lack the proper order God established. Time and years, do not move the precepts of God. What He established in the beginning, is still the standard for our marriages today.

The trouble is, man and woman have attempted to change the ways, rules and standards of God; for an institution that doesn't belong to them. An institution they are only privileged to enter into.

We don't change the rules of God. If we decide to enter into marriage; we go by His rules or marriage isn't for us. I couldn't tell my manager that I was changing my performance standards. I had to measure up to them! I had to follow the guidelines and precepts set for me. Our marriages are no different!

In order to do this, you must move away from the world. You must set your sites on the scriptures; rather than the TV. What people in the world are doing, how they're acting; is of no concern to us. They're

MY NAME IS LOVE

waiting for us to be light and salt to them! We can never be until we align our hearts with truth and obedience.

Through this word; God is setting you free from the slavery of deceit and blindness. Walk towards the light! Your lives, marriages and families, will open up like you've never seen before. You taking your place, will allow your husband to take his. Order will be established in your home and marriage and with it; great joy and delight.

You've been missing out because you've tried to take matters into your own hands, through your own strength. God's ways are not our ways! Things work when we follow His order and commands. Relinquish your control, and allow your man to lead through your encouragement.

There's nothing the husband of the wife in Proverbs wouldn't do for her, because she sought good for him always. In his comfort, he blessed, praised and honored her! Any man will bend over backwards, and do flips for his wife, if she respects and honors him. The secret isn't control! It's letting go of your ways for God's. The Bible says… "If you cling to your life, you will lose it; but if you give up your life for me, you will find it." Matthew 10:39

Desire to be this woman for God. Your mind and body will move you towards your desire. Don't even do it for your husband! You will automatically be this for him… From the residuals of your obedience to God!

Ladies, now that you know your performance standards… Don't just meet them! Exceed them in reverence to God! You'll live a life you've always dreamed of… And greater!

Chapter 9

GOD›S MAN

~ A man's strength is not measured by what he destroys... But by what he Builds! By the lives he impacts for good; not detriment! ~

GOD'S MAN

Let me be a man! Let me cover you in my care. Let me do for you as far as my imagination extends. Let me rescue you from the false and the foolishness. Come to me, free to indulge in the delight of being... Woman, loved and seen through different eyes.

I see as I'm seen. I now know differently. Let me be the conduit; the expression of His love towards you in human form. Let me be the nexus; the link, to show how to love you as required of a man.

You are my gift from God, clothed in the shape of woman. Only you could bring out what God has hidden inside of me. You give me expression. You enlarge the chambers of my heart. You are why my arms were given strength... To hold you, to protect you; to support you.

You are in no way weak. My support is in addition to your strength. My strength is not in opposition to yours; but complementary. We give each

MY NAME IS LOVE

other together what we would never find alone. We are unique as one. We are transcendent together.

Our lives woven together as one entity; to defy the Laws of Physics. We are union. We are set apart in purpose. Greatness now gravitates towards us as we have stepped into our place ordained before time. We are one, together with God and Universe to attract, draw and deliver what is good and light to others.

Let others bask in the glow of our amazement. Let them desire to walk in light and purpose as we have chosen. Let them abandon self and shadow; and take upon the mantle of togetherness. Let them take of our light and ignite it in others.

Open eyes and hearts through our display Lord. Give desire to all that see. Give awareness that this is the way; not the ways they've been traveling along; broken and dusty roads. Come to the light of His hand extended as freedom.

I desire to be all to you; for you. My ways have been changed to fit you precisely. My heart has been modified to please, to protect and to provide security and safety within my realm. I cherish the position of responsibility. With gladness, I accept the title of husband bestowed upon me through the Institution of God. I am privileged to wear it. It deepens my thoughts and awareness to become much more than I ever was alone.

I see the world through different eyes. I am not alone. I have been given the privilege of responsibility of another life. God has entrusted me with His own creation. It's an awesome obligation; not to be taken lightly or for granted.

I will walk in this forever… Seeking His hand to guide us in His purpose and direction.

MEN IDENTIFY YOURSELVES

Stand up and stand out! Separate yourself! Pull yourself away from the crowd and be on God's team. God is calling for men today to separate yourself from the world. To separate from the ways of the world. To separate from the thoughts and mannerisms of the world... To be right, and to do things right. He's calling men to be responsible and accountable. He's calling us to take our rightful places in society, in our marriages, in our homes, and with our children.

Who out there will take a stand for God and say 'I AM SUCH A MAN!' Who out there will identify himself as such a man to a women looking for a good man. A man not into playing games with her heart and emotions. And if she's right for you, you will honor her in the bonds of marriage, commitment and love.

Who will identify himself by stepping out, and standing out from the rest of the world whose gamin, playin, thuggin, pimpin and treating women wrong. Who will stand up and say... 'I am such a man who sincerely loves and honors God. I will honor you, by serving you and your needs before my own. I will never degrade you by sending you to work, while I stay home and did nothing. I will honor you by having my own place to bring you to after we're married. Even if it's a small, but adequate place. It will be ours until I can do better... But we will not live with my parents.'

We as men must identify ourselves as serious men wanting to do the will of God with one woman heading towards marriage. For too long, women have seen the wrong kind of man; and have adjusted her impression of bad as good and attractive. God has nothing in that. It's called deceit. It's a game that Satan plays to destroy you as women, and the lives of the children you give life to. Satan has deceived you for too long. He's told you that the bad guy was what's happening. Although he treated you like crap, disrespected you, and dishonored you, and you still

MY NAME IS LOVE

fell for it. A sincere man who loved God approached you without all the nonsense, treating you like a lady; and you dismissed him as weak!

Ladies, Satan has deceived you to believe a lie just like Eve in the garden. It's no different! God has brought you right, and you pushed it away as wrong for you. Satan brought you wrong, and you accepted it with open arms. There's something wrong with that picture!

God is calling men to stand up and take our places. God is calling women to wise up and no longer be deceived by the men that come to you. You won't get anything good from something bad. The Bible tells us not to partner with those who are unsaved or we'll find ourselves "unequally yoked," in a bond for life suffering, and crying out to God for help! We'll be asking why we allowed ourselves to get into such a mess.

God sent us this word to warn us. As a matter of fact, I was soaking in my hot tub when He spoke these words to me. I knew what that meant... Get out; and start writing as He speaks! It's just that important!

THE INITIATORS

Today man is confused and doesn't know his place. Some have even tried to do right before God in being the leaders of their homes, but went to take their place as God ordained... But found someone else in his place of leadership... The Woman!

As a result of knowing who God made him, and who God assigned him to be in his home, the man stands confused and out of his place. He may even try to take his place, but his woman is in his seat. He feels awkward and uncomfortable, and can never be the man God created him to be outside of his proper role. But actually it's not the woman's fault... It's the man's!

GOD'S MAN

Its not the specific man, but the general man over time as a whole. Through time, man has not seen women in the light as God intended him to see her... As a gift designed specifically just for him. With such a precious, priceless gift from God, man would have to be a fool to abuse it. And he has!

Through time, ignorant man has failed to realized the treasure he was given by God. Instead of holding and embracing her closely, he arrogantly attempted to put her under his feet to control her, belittle her, and degrade her as less than equal.

Ladies let's make this clear again, GOD MADE YOU EQUAL, MAN MADE YOU LESS! God had nothing to do with the treatment you received from man. Only your roles in the bonds of marriage would be different under the headship and order of God. Even there, we as men are required to submit our lives unto death for you as Christ did. Now that's love! There's no abuse, neglect, degradation whatsoever in this requirement.

The problem is our ancestors didn't do right by our women, and over time; women took enough abuse, and came up swinging. They determined within themselves to never be abused and controlled again by a man. They became angry, and bitter in their determination.

Women went into marriages with this same attitude to never be controlled by their husbands. It was a 'Wall of Society' that she bought into. She took those walls and defenses into her marriage. The man thought he was marrying a sweet flower. Who he married was a business executive determined to run things her way.

Society told her to take her place as the head before the man could take it. If he did, she used her strategy on him... Her body! A woman knows a man is attracted to every inch of her body, and she can wrongly use this against the man to control and degrade him.

MY NAME IS LOVE

She knows just how to pick a non existent fight to put a man on the couch, and have him sitting there with his head spinning; wondering what just happened. She knows how to use the headache routine, and the fake monthly cycle to push him away; knowing he wants to be with her. She knows how to give in just a little bit, just as a concession. He gives up a part of himself, and part of his manhood, as he's made to grovel for something God gave him for free in marriage. She uses her two greatest weapons to move the man from his seat of leadership as God ordained. She's used the two most powerful gifts she's been given by God to comfort her husband. But she's used them to tear him down and degrade him instead. These two precious gifts are… Her body and her words.

With her words, she builds her man up to believe he can defeat the world for her. With her body, she seals the deal! Satan has got into the marriage over the years, where he has no business. Marriage is the institution of God. Satan deployed this strategy through women to wreak havoc and destruction in our marriages. And the sad thing is, out of ignorance, we've fallen for it.

To fix this, we as men of this generation; must make this right. Our forefathers, and we too; are responsible. None of us are exempt! All of us must make it right.

Now that God has revealed the problem to us, we as men must humbly and with apology, take our places in our homes as God has ordained. Regardless of the wrong we did yesterday, this is a new day. Apologize and move forward.

The walls our wives built were out of protection, and to survive from our foolish ways. Now she doesn't need them. She was only waiting for us to take our rightful place. As a woman, she didn't design herself, nor was she designed by man… She is God's handiwork, created from man's body; to help us fulfill our assignments from God.

GOD'S MAN

A woman will only fulfill the purpose God created her for, doing what God assigned her... Where He assigned her. Otherwise, she'll live an empty, unfulfilled existence. Still there are some that desire neither relationship or marriage. This is for the ones who desire to be married.

We as men are the initiators! We've made things wrong, and must be the facilitators to make things right once more. By taking our rightful places as head of the household in humility and love; under the leadership of God... Our wives will take hers. We must cover her with love, concern, unselfishness, commitment and responsibility. We must be demonstrators and not just talkers.

Taking our places will allow the Societal Wall the woman has brought into the marriage, to fall and crumble. Then, both husband and wife can take their proper roles before God in marriage.

A MAN'S ROLE DEFINED

God says today's man is confused and doesn't know his role. If he doesn't know his proper role, then how can he ever fill it!

The role of a man is of both Angel & Soldier! He must be as gentle as an Angel, but as strong, firm and protective as a soldier. He must be both. The wise man knows when to be both from spending time with God, and seeking His wisdom through His word.

For example, as an angel a man displays love for his woman by rubbing her feet and hands, taking her to the spa to unwind, taking her out for a nice romantic dinner and having her flowers waiting for her at their table. He demonstrates his love for her through acts of kindness.

On the other hand, when his wife comes home after listening to her single girlfriend's fill her head with a bunch of foolishness and she

MY NAME IS LOVE

starts acting crazy… The man must now become the soldier. He must stand as God has made him to stand, and explain to his wife that… 'Honey, we serve God in this house, and we obey His order for our marriage. Not the world's! Satan I rebuke you in the name of Jesus! You must leave this house! We're servants of God! You, women's lib, or any other order is not welcome here. God is Head of this household. It's His Kingdom that reigns, and His order that rules here!'

When we've grown to that point as Christians, we've reached maturity, and we'll see the Christian divorce rate stop climbing. We'll also begin to see the world's divorce rate stop climbing… Because we'll finally have taken our rightful places as LIGHT AND SALT TO THEM as God ordained us to be!

REAL MEN ARE DOING; BEING… NOT SAYING

The purity in my motive, of caring for you… Compelled through love and obedience to God. The more I love God, the more I love you. The more I love God, the deeper I cherish you.

I've transferred the limits of my earthly love, to one that's supernatural. To one which exceeds my own expectations, and my imagination. I no longer desire to walk in foolishness. Such things fall off in the presence of God; in the will and purpose of God. I desire to be all scheduled, planned, ordained and predestined for you; in our Holy union before God and the world.

The spark of my obedience to God produces light in our union, in our family, and in the world. God endows us with light to draw others to it. Others run to it in thirst; desperate for a drink of it.

Tired of their struggles. Tired of foolishness and insecurities. People are crying out to God… 'Please, I'm trying to do right, but this is too

GOD'S MAN

much! I didn't get married for this foolishness! I never signed up for this mess.' With hands pointed towards Heaven; they surrender!

Surrender is a victory flag for God! Surrender isn't a ditch, it's a bridge that leads to our salvation. Surrender isn't the end, it's the beginning of a new direction. It's a new walk, with meaning and purpose.

Awareness has come! Through the eyes of awareness; clarity. Through clarity comes alignment. The alignment of my will with God's. With the alignment of my will, there's a change in my choices; my decisions and my views. These changes produce a difference in my habits, personality and character.

Where I was once living in shadow, I'm now standing in the light. This is where foolishness falls off of me. Bad habits run away from me. Desires are deleted within me. I've given up through gain! I've let go and prospered. I've surrendered and won!

Victory and joy are words now common to me. I walk in them with gladness and thanksgiving. I've been changed! I'm alive and living. I affect lives and environment around me for good. I Influence situations and circumstances for better. Yet still, I have the humility and awareness to know that the influence and effectiveness is God; not I.

This is who I am now. I've been given a new mandate; a new decree of change. I'll walk in it. My conversation will be different as a result of it. I no longer want what I use to. Now, when I look in the mirror, I just don't see my own reflection. I see the reflection of others beside me and all around me. Their lives were always connected to mine. They were always in the mirror where I stood. The shadow in my life hid them from my awareness. I didn't know they were there!

Now I see them. My gifts are for them. My purpose propels me to them, and them to me. Now they walk in light instead of shadow.

They now become… Instruments of change around them.

MY NAME IS LOVE

BECAUSE OF HER

Who is he because of her. How is his potential maximized! He's free. Free to be who God created him to be. He discovers things about himself he would never had known without her. He see's his path clearer. She's an illuminator! She enlightens, for him to see. He now understands his reason and being.

Because she holds it down for him, he can focus on his career and his life purpose. He takes his place in his career, and in the community. He sits amongst the elders. He walks with a feeling of security, knowing she wants the best in life for him. The Bible tells us in Proverbs... "She does good for him; not evil, all the days of his life." Proverbs 31:12

Because of all she is to him, he thrives. For this, he praises her. He adores her. He realizes he's blessed because of her. He cherishes her, and never takes her for granted. He knows it's not always so with other men and marriages. He could look around and see he was allowed to be different. All because of her.

She's unique! She's special! The fear; the respect and reverence she has for God, causes her to be this remarkable woman. All she does is unto God. Her husband gleans from the residuals of her obedience, and true relationship with God.

She doesn't walk in conflict or chaos. She walks in the light of purpose. This keeps her focused, and away from the ways and mannerisms of the world and others.

She's not influenced by other women. She's the influencer! She influences them. She sets her own standards according to the precepts of God. She influences her children. She's light to all she comes in contact with. The reputation of her goes before her and beyond her. She influences those she will never see or know.

The Bible says… "He who finds a wife finds a good thing and obtains favor from the LORD." Proverbs 18:22

He is… Because of her!

I'VE NEVER NOT LOVED ANITA BAKER

It was one of those sayings that would come to my mind. I didn't know what it meant.

Today, I would find out! I've always loved Anita Baker; the epitome of class, smoothness and elegance. She sings with a voice so true and refined. One note transverses into the next; without effort or chore. She touches my soul deeply in her effervescence.

Today I saw something absolutely incredible. It was a short video tribute to honor Ms. Baker on YouTube. In the video, the announcer says… "Ladies and gentlemen; Mr. El DeBarge!"

He came to honor her… Her works, her voice; her contributions to life and music.

There he came on the stage. The man was clean; impeccably dressed. Not a hair out of place… Smooth personified. His voice impeccable; drawing Ms. Baker to put her shoes back on, to come up on the stage; to be in his presence. Walking in his gift, he serenaded her with her own song in smoothness.

Beauty to behold… Smoothness and the Songstress; bringing indelible light to countless!

This man inspires me; and I, keep the pedal to the floor. I dress; and pride myself in my attitude and appearance. But this man inspires me to step it up… Higher & Further! Whenever I see him, I'm checking my hair; my look. I'm not jealous of the man. I appreciate him! Come to me in smoothness and sharpness! I want to see it; because it inspires me even more to reach for higher heights. To you… Mr. El DeBarge, Sir; I say thank you!

As men today, what examples do we have of men. Where are the men who inspire us to dress, to carry ourselves with class and dignity. Who inspires us to greatness!

As men; why can't we be happy for men! Why can't we praise them when we see them shining in their lights! Why must we hate, if they're doing something; being someone different than us. I'm happy when I see others doing well. I'm happy for them!

Most of us as men aren't. It's that mentality that I don't want you surpassing me in anything. So stay in your lane and we'll be cool! It's shallowness at its height. It's jealousy at it's peak. A man who walks in these things, only happy for himself, fails to see the fullness of God. Although he says he knows God; he really doesn't.

For if he knew God; he would know these words that would have rid him of his hating on others, his jealousy and his resentment. He would know this… God has All things infinitely. What He gives to me doesn't diminish His supply one iota.

He has stood wrongly in his jealousy! Come to the light and walk in freedom!

I SEE…

I see my wife and my marriage completely different. As the man and husband, I must take the lead in Life, Love & Purpose. I must model for her an example of love, so she can reciprocate, magnify and multiply love to me. But I must be the initiator. I must take the lead in making effort.

It's my requirement as a man.

ASKING TO BE LED

To lead is an incredible privilege and responsibility. The greatest of leaders are selfless. They know the mantle of leadership requires them to put others above themselves. You are the greatest, and the least of the equation. You don't lead with self in mind. Your leadership requires you to put your needs at the back of the line... So the needs of those you lead remain paramount.

WHERE ARE THE MEN FOR US

Who models manhood and responsibility for us. So many come from broken homes without a dad around to teach them. Mom can't teach us how to be a man. Only a man can do that.

Who do we see that comes close to being an example for us. We definitely can't look to TV for our examples. Where does this leave us; floundering, not knowing how to be the best products of ourselves as men. It leaves us mostly, just getting by and modeling that before our children. And sadly, the cycle continues. We don't want just 'getting by,' we want excellence!

Fortunately for me, I have an example of a man in my life. No, he's not my father. He's my spiritual big brother.

If you take the word 'many' and remove the 'm,' it leaves us with the word 'any.' It's not that I know many men like him... I don't know 'Any' men like him!

MY NAME IS LOVE

He's a man's man; with a servants heart. He tossed his pride away many years ago to be a servant. He cherishes his role, and it's a beautiful thing to see.

Most men don't know how to treat a lady. Most of us were never shown, nor showed any interest in learning. His servant's heart taught him how.

This man cooks; not hot dogs, but meals. He cleans the house. He loads the dishwasher. He does whatever's needed to meet the needs of his family.

He has one of the most imaginative and creative minds I've ever seen. The events he plans for his wife and others are simply amazing.

I study him. I learn from him. He teaches me and so many others by his example of selflessness and servanthood. Most of us men are so full of pride; these things are beneath us. Showing love; expressing it constantly and sincerely, are just not things we deem important and necessary. But they're essential in a successful relationship; especially marriage.

He's held it down for 46 years of marriage. One of the last times I talked to him, he was cooking catfish for dinner. He was cooking another type of fish for his wife. Another time I talked to him, he had taken his wife to Monterey for vacation.

He's full of ideas, initiative and love. This man loves unashamed, and absent of pride. It's such an amazing thing to see.

He takes the lead by example. He cares less what the world thinks of him; he's being light and salt to them.

We need him as men, to show us the way; to model a servant's heart, absent of pride. There's nothing too high out of his reach, nor anything too low beneath him to accomplish. He's a man's man absent of pride, and an incredible example we all need as men.

Thank you my big brother... Mr. Alvin McGary!

TODAY I HAD THE PRIVILEGE

Today I had the privilege to talk to my wife. The privilege to talk to her on the phone. To talk to her by video. To talk to her for over two hours.

You may say... .What's the big deal! Privileges can be something restored to us. They can be things we have, and recognize as blessings and opportunities in our life. Privileges are also things we can lose due to blindness, neglect and things we take for granted that they'll just be there for us without any effort or imagination.

Having such things and having my sight restored; I never want to be without them again. Simple things such as a text, a phone call; a conversation.

Loss has a way of awakening us to truth. Loss can take us on a path of clarity where we realize that complaint, blame and lack of contentment, were all liars to lead us astray, to the land of nothingness. That land of barrenness and emptiness, where shallowness and selfishness reside in splendor. With a little insight, a little effort and much appreciation, I would have never discovered this desolate place. But for pride and arrogance, I slipped over into nothingness. A land I dare not visit again, through the efforts of appreciation, gratitude and thankfulness.

So you say... What's the big deal, you got to talk to your wife today. I would rather you take my word and learn from it, than to slip over into nothingness and emptiness and find out for yourself.

Chapter 10

LIFE & DEATH FROM OUR MOUTHS

~ Our World's take the Shape of the things we Speak! ~

WITH THE INTENT TO HURT

Let's be real… You said that with the intent to hurt!

The Bible says… "Death and life are in the power of the tongue." Proverbs 18:21 And "Let no corrupt talk come out of your mouths, but only what is good for edifying." Ephesians 4:29 The Bible describes the tongue as a small member of the body, and likens it to the smallest of rudder on a great ship, which can move such a large vessel through wind and seas. It refers to it as the smallest spark, which can set a mighty forrest to blaze. In other words, the Bible is telling us… The tongue although small, can do great good or tremendous damage!

Let's make something clear… Love never fails! When we hurt and do harm to others, we have walked out of love. Love isn't capable of such things. So what causes us to step out of love?

Fear and hurt will cause us to vacate our positions. So, to prevent us from moving from our assigned places; we need to address what triggers fear and hurt within us, and be proactive; rather than reactive in our relationships.

LIFE & DEATH FROM OUR MOUTHS

All of us are damaged in some ways. Especially those of us that have been in bad relationships. They can do tremendous harm and destruction to our hearts, minds, and our outlook on life and others.

Before we enter a relationship, we should take inventory of our hearts. We must search ourselves for bitterness, pain and unforgiveness left over from past relationships. Write them down; confess them. Pray about them. But get them out of your heart and mind.

Don't go loaded with a bitter heart in a clean relationship. Start fresh! Release the ghost of your past. This is not that person which stands before you. Don't compare them with anyone. They didn't do what others did, and they deserve to live or die on their own merits.

In marriage; communication is one of your most important tools. Tell each other your triggers… 'When you do this it hurts, or I'm afraid when this happens.' Remove the unknowns. Being ignorant or unaware can be damaging. We're not known for talking sensibly about our issues. What we do is yell, scream and holler, when our buttons are pushed.

We must identify, name and claim these buttons. Put a label on them, to make them clear. Know them; memorize them, and discuss ways to eliminate them together. We'll find out we weren't the monsters others thought we were… We were just stepping on land mines Unaware!

This wisdom from God can save our marriages. It's something the enemy doesn't want you to know. He'd rather you stay ignorant to his devices to separate and divide you. By the way, this is his strategy to ruin your marriage… To separate and divide you through hurt and fear produced arguments. His goal is to turn you on each other, and step aside while you fight, argue and destroy your lives and marriage.

These arguments lead to the lack of communication. The lack of communication leads to unfiltered thoughts. These thoughts get carried away in our imaginations, thinking things are worse than they are. All of this can be avoided by identifying, naming and claiming our stressors.

Once we confess out loud to each other what these stressors are that trigger us going off… We must bury them, and not use them again to hurt each other. The problem with some people is; vulnerability. Some people don't like to expose their hearts. Let me ask you this… How can you be in a marriage based on love if you have trouble exposing your heart! It can be pride! It can be fear of hurt.

We must use these tools God has given us today to fix and remedy our fears and insecurities. Those aren't things we should have with the person we promised to love until death departed us.

We must change! We must change now; not tomorrow! The world is in a broken state because of our failed marriages. Even us as Christians are failing in our marriages, just like the ones in the world. It's because we don't deal with the issues in our hearts. We react to them rather than respond. Now we can respond with wisdom, rather than with arguments and anger.

No more crossing boundaries that have been mutually established! No more bringing up sensitive issues that hurt. Until we bring these issues into the light; they'll still be sensitive.

Be strong! Deal with them openly and together! Don't be ashamed to confess your weaknesses. Provide a safe environment for sharing such things without judgement or repercussions.

God desires our marriages to be healed. No more foolishness, and going off about small things. Be aware of the lines, and don't cross them in love. Gone are the days of hurting each other with the intent to do damage. Gone are the days of insecurities of 'I'll hurt you before, or because you hurt me.'

LIFE & DEATH FROM OUR MOUTHS

These are the days to put all of that foolishness aside. Grow; mature in your relationship and marriage, so you're an example for your children, and light and salt to those around you.

Put the hurt aside. No longer be a hurt person that hurts people because your heart is damaged. Fix your heart by releasing those painful stressors, through confessing and addressing them.

It's time that we that confess Christ; display it in our lives, through obedience and humility. It's time that our marriages no longer resemble the world's, and take on the light and wisdom of Christ!

> "TJ. Those words are a gift from God. I'm not trying to say they couldn't be yours; but the shining truth and love in the words, not to mention the wisdom and God's Providence. God is speaking through you. I have known many people who say God is giving them their words, but in reality it doesn't seem so. You- it is clear God speaks to/through you! It is amazing, TJ! What a blessing!"

Debra D'Attoma

WORDS NOT AS WEAPONS BUT AS MAGNIFIERS

"The wise woman builds her house [on a foundation of godly precepts, and her household thrives], But the foolish one [who lacks spiritual insight] tears it down with her own hands [by ignoring godly principles]." Proverbs 14:1

The woman doesn't physically tear down her house. The house still stands; but in disarray! She doesn't physically demolish it with her hands. She does it with her Words & Attitude!

MY NAME IS LOVE

The Bible illustrates to us that a woman's greatest strength isn't in her hands... It's in her words! Through them, she edifies or demolishes. Through them, she praises or puts down.

God made us different; man and woman. He made us each unique to certain skill sets and abilities. He made us strong in areas; not so strong in others. Even Adam; Earth's first perfect man, had his limitations. Even a perfect man, God looked upon him and saw the need for a woman in his life. We are no different today thousands of years later.

We as Adam, long for that woman in our lives. We long for her companionship, we long for her comfort. She gives us what we wouldn't have without her. She brings to us an abundance of what we couldn't discover alone.

Where we lack, she gains. Where we're weak, she's strong. Where we lack vision, she sees. She's a help in our shortcomings. She's a bridge in our gaps. She helps us be who we were designed to be by God. She gives us a platform, to perform the purpose assigned by God upon our lives and families. She came to us with great reason and purpose. Her presence was designed by God to unite; to unify the family towards a spiritual goal. She gives a man pride, reason; drive to fulfill the purpose God assigned upon his life. She's many things. God designed her as such.

It was God, not man, that designed man. It was God that placed certain things common to all men. A man desires to lead. He desires to protect. He desires to work with his hands or his mind. He first; was created in the image and likeness of God. Therefore, as God desires to be praised and lifted up, so does a man within limits.

It's called his ego. It can easily be edified or bruised. It can motivate him to move mountains. It can slow him to a crawl. It's not something man gave himself. It was given to him by God; in His design. Who can argue with the Hand of God!

LIFE & DEATH FROM OUR MOUTHS

His ego is the key to his engine ladies. You feed it, he'll do incredible things for you, himself, his family and others. Starve it, he'll wander aimlessly; looking for his purpose in life.

Life is in our words. Proverbs tells us that… "Life and death are in the power of the tongue." Proverbs 18:21 A woman, small in frame and stature, can destroy the largest man. Look at Samson! He was the strongest man to ever live. He was destroyed through the words of a woman.

Today, more than ever, we need to recognize and know these truths of God for our marriages and families. The divorce rate for Christians is just as high as worldly marriages. It shouldn't be! We've lost our way, and have abandoned the truths and principles of God. We have followed the world's ways, instead of being light and salt to it; as we're supposed to be.

In the garden, Adam could have still lived forever, after his wife ate of the forbidden fruit. Even after she ate, he was still eternal. The command of God was given to the man. The Bible tell us in Genesis 2:16-17 that… "And the LORD God commanded the man, saying, Of every tree of the garden you may freely eat: But of the tree of the knowledge of good and evil, you shalt not eat of it: for in the day that you eat thereof you shall surely die." This command was given to the man before the woman was created. It tells us this… Responsibility was given to the man for his actions, and later for his family. He would be held accountable for both. God would come to him, not the woman; for the order of his family.

We as men, one day will give an account to God for our families; not the wife. Her accountability will be how well, or how she didn't support him in the governing of the family.

MY NAME IS LOVE

One is accountable for overall. One is accountable for support. Our success or failure lies within the Words of our mouths!

Will we use our words as weapons or magnifiers! If life and death are in the power of our words… Then how much more are they the success or failure of our marriages and families!

It's time we stop following the ways of the world, and start following the commands and principles of God!

ONE OF YOU

One of you has to be the mediator! The one with the calm voice. The one to bring things back to center.

One of you has to be the calm one. One of you has to see the bigger picture. One of you must be able to reason.

You must learn to fight fairly. You must look with reason to be grateful, rather than to complain. An argument is a losing situation. No one wins! Voices are raised. Boiling points are reached. Situations get out of hand. Situations remain the same… Or worse!

Instead of arguing… Say what you mean! State the real issue. The issue between the lines; hidden within an argument.

What's this argument really about! Is it about something that's happening now, or is it a trigger for something built up from the past! How can we solve what we don't know. How can we address what's hidden!

Is this even a real argument, or is it an excuse to go off! Is it a reason to scold; because you're in a bad mood, or you lack self control!

Because I'm near you; am I your whipping board! What the world, or others has done to you; I have no part in. Are you haunted by your past! Have I been something that reminded you of your pain of the past! Is there hurt, not dealt with, in you that causes you to lash out at me. Am I your whipping board! No, I'm not!

Can something so minor trigger something so large. This is me today; standing before you with one wrong; one incident. Does it solicit such!

Too many times we carryover our past into our present. It's good for neither of us; our relationship, or our marriage. We must deal only with the person which stands before us. Not the ghost of others, for which we haven't repented.

An argument is rooted in hurt or fear. Instead of labeling the person before us, who stands with the solution and remedy… We should just tell them the Truth! 'Baby,when you said this to me… It hurt!' 'Love, when you act like this… I'm afraid I'm going to lose you!' When you open a dialogue like that, it leads to conversation and mediation. But the way we've been handling our arguments, it leads to more damage and pain; leaving the real root issue still unresolved.

We must come off of our pride, and speak what's really bothering us. We must watch how we address things. Starting off accusing the person doesn't work. It puts them in a defensive mode, where they're now guarding their feelings and emotions.

We must learn to cut our voices; lower our tones and speak in non offensives. We must seek to start a dialogue; not a monologue. The best solutions are reached when both provide input and problem solving.

And ladies, please don't do the craziest thing some of you do… Argue because of peace! Some people argue just because things are going good.

MY NAME IS LOVE

They pick a fight out of the blue, and the man is totally confused as to what is going on. Five minutes ago, he had a peaceful home.

Is this also done out of fear. Is fear the real issue here. Are you afraid because things have been going well for a while; you fear the blessing given to you; so you attempt to sabotage it? How crazy is that!

The Bible tells us to renew our minds. We must rid our minds of hurt and fear. We must rid them of our ghost of past hurts through bad relationships, and replace that with forgiveness, peace, thanks and gratitude.

A king or a queen given to you by God, stands before you. Don't reduce them to a pauper, from your hidden hurts and insecurities; through the uselessness of arguing!

CROSS OVER INTO SILENCE

Men and women are different. Especially in arguments. The mind of a woman can run circles around a man, and leave us wondering what just happened. A woman knows she has this advantage over a man. Some women even drag men into this realm on purpose to control and manipulate them. This is not the effective use of a gift. It's taking something God has given you for good, and using it illegitimately.

A woman can use this to tear down, to belittle; to do damage and harm to her man. Here, she's king! But a good woman doesn't tear down her husband with her words. She lifts him up, and edifies him as God intended her to do.

Where does this leave us in the realm of arguing? It leaves us to sticking to the issue. One issue; not going back in time and adding on things of the past. And the real issue too! Speak the truth in love without pride. If a man was late, don't start off with… 'You're always!' No one is 'Always.' The one time we're not that thing, we disqualify for being Always!

Lay it down right. Say… 'It's important to me that you're on time.' It's more appropriate, non offensive and non threatening. If you begin by labeling a man, telling him who he is and what he isn't… You're going to get silence from him.

God gave a man an ego, just like he gave the woman the ability to reason and analyze. When we feel threatened and don't have the tools to compete… We shut down! We've been put in a world where we're an alien. We're unfamiliar with feeling inadequate, and not knowing what to say. When our ego is attacked, to prevent further damage; we disengage from the situation. This is not the proper place to take someone you love over an argument.

Sure we'll have arguments and disagreements in marriage. But we must know the rules. We must know that most women will naturally have the advantage, because her minds works differently than a man's. Where she can think of multiple things at a time. Men think of one. We're not on her level in this department. A woman can easily manipulate to control; because we lack in this arena. It doesn't means she's right. It just means she can outmaneuver us in this area.

Stick to the issue! Seek a mutual solution that works for both of you. Definitely, and I mean definitely; leave the labeling out. It will shut a man down instantly. He will disengage mentally, or walk away physically. You'll end up sleeping on the farthest side of the bed that night. If you can sleep at all!

Take the wisdom that God has given you this day ladies. Know in arguing, you have a huge advantage over your husband. God gave you those skills to help, not for destruction, or to tear down your man.

Know these things, and don't allow the enemy to take you places you shouldn't be. A simple argument can lead to much more, and cause damage if not handled properly. Use the tools God gave you... The sweetness of your voice; your gentleness!

Use them to edify and build... Not for destruction!

ALWAYS

Can any of us say we're 'Always!' Are any of us even entitled to use the word. Can we label others with it.

Always means continuously; every time we do something. None of us are always! The one time we aren't, the one time our behavior doesn't coincide with that condition; we disqualify for always.

We are not always loving. We are not always kind. We are not always patient. We're human beings with a sinful nature. We can never qualify for always. We can never reach its standards.

When we argue, when we criticize and say... 'You always do that, or you're always like that.' We're wrong! Whether good or bad... We can not be always!

Only God Himself qualifies for Always! He alone is absolute! He, nor anything about Him ever changes. Where we are not; He is always loving, kind and patient. He is always everything that's good. Even in his correction and admonition; He always does it in love. There's never a time that He's not always.

Only God... Is Always!

LIFE & DEATH FROM OUR MOUTHS

THE VOLUME OF YOUR VOICE

The volume of your voice doesn't make it true.

The volume of your voice doesn't make you right. The volume of your voice doesn't make your lies correct. The volume of your voice doesn't change my mind. It just places me in silence; waiting for you to finish talking.

The volume of your voice doesn't make you wise or accurate. It doesn't mean you're strong. You didn't win the argument! I forfeited just to keep you quiet. You didn't shut me up. I shut myself up, because I no longer wanted to hear you speak. If anything, it means you're demonstrating weakness from the lack of restraint, and self control of your emotions.

The volume of your voice is a weapon to attempt to distract me from the real issue. You try to exchange loudness for confusion.

The loudness of your voice is your emotions unhinged; unharnessed. Its just voice without substance. It's just beating the air. It's just the vibrating of vocal chords. All music is not song. All conversation; not meaningful.

Seek substance over volume. Seek wisdom over air.

Whether you realize it or not, the loudness of your voice speaks volumes about you!

Chapter 11

A WILLINGNESS TO CHANGE

~ THE TRANSITION...

Now you love the person; rather than just the image. ~

A WILLINGNESS TO CHANGE

One thing we leave out of the newness of our marriage is that we must have... A willingness to change!

Two separate lives joined together as one. Two different backgrounds. Different values and views on life. Raised in different families. Living in different parts of the country. This is not a recipe for an unwillingness to change.

Love requires that we must be willing to give up parts of ourselves, to gain in others. Two main things we can't carry into marriage is Selfishness & Pride! These are two of the most destructive behaviors in life. We can't afford them to enter into our marriages with us.

One of the problems is when we enter marriage, we believed we've reach the finish line. When in actuality... We're just beginning!

A WILLINGNESS TO CHANGE

Compromise is key. One of us shouldn't have our way all of the time. Love gives. Love is unselfish. Love places others before ourselves. Love leaves room for ideas, suggestions and recommendations from another. We incorporate; we don't monopolize in love.

We bend, we flex; we bow in praise to God for giving us a life partner. We bless Him that we're not left alone in the foolishness of this world today, with its looseness and temptations. We're thankful to God that we find our needs in the One He's given us through marriage.

Because we're thankful, we put our pride and selfishness aside to do what it takes to meet the needs of the one we love. Those vows we took weren't just for the wedding day. They were for life!

Our marriage, and life ever evolving; we must remain flexible to change. We can't remain that person they married! We must be better! What we got through dating and at the wedding, should have been only a sample of who we are. God doesn't expect instant satisfaction from us just because we marry. He requires that satisfaction to grow continuously through our willingness to be pliable, flexible, bendable and through our ability to stretch, see things differently; and adapt.

Marriage will take us places, and teach us things we would have never known without it. We experience the love of God physically through that person. But God also uses this leverage of love, that we have for each other, to change and mature us. The problem here is when God begins to do this, the inexperienced couple begins to blame each other, instead of realizing that's it's just a natural progression of God's institution of marriage.

Within His institution, He requires that we learn, we grow, we give up things; we deposit some of those behaviors we've held on to and put them in the trash. God will identify them through marriage.

Don't blame your spouse! It's not them bringing out the worse in you! It's God ridding you of extra baggage you've been carrying for years. He now has your attention through the leverage of love in your marriage. Besides; you promised not to go anywhere! So you're now in the circumference of marriage which requires change.

This is another area the enemy will try to trick us and attempt to destroy our marriage. When God, not your spouse, begins to put His finger on those unyielded ares you've been hiding, covering and disguising… It causes us to see how ugly we are inside… The first thing we'll do is lash out and blame our spouse. The first words out of our mouths will be… 'You bring out the worst in me! I was never like this before I married you!'

The truth is, you were like that and worse! You've been hiding those dark qualities of your personality. You didn't display them while dating, or you would have ran the person off. So you concealed them. They've peek their head out at times through arguments, tantrums, or when you've lost restraint and self control. They've been there through sharp barbs, and arrows you've thrown. They've always been there, and will remain; if God doesn't remove them.

We can't hold on to our old selves in marriage. We must throw away that old phrase… 'You knew how I was when you married me. Don't expect me to change!' Unacceptable! God requires you to change! We don't get married to sit down on our morals. This is the place in our lives where we're most responsible! This is the place where we become responsible for our personalities and behaviors; as we vowed this to God during the wedding ceremony.

This is your time. Marriage is your season to be free of such destructive traits and ways. God loves you, and doesn't want to leave you like that. Now that you've moved into the realm of His Institution of marriage, He can begin to free you from yourself through the love of the person

A WILLINGNESS TO CHANGE

you married. And the best part besides the freedom is; you have that person to love you, and be there with you through it!

Seeing ourselves naked; without the clothes of our looks, our bodies, our jobs, money, titles and positions… Is scary! All these props we lean on, make us who we think we are. This is not the real 'Us,' in the eyes of God. He sees us fully naked in all of our ways, and the ones we try to hide from others. We must give into the change!

It's guaranteed to happen, so we must be prepared for it. Through this process, God removes the darkness from our hearts, so our lights will shine brightly. Here, we become a lighthouse to draw others to Him.

Accept the beauty through maturity God gives to us through change. It will bless our marriages and our lives immensely!

YOU MUST FIRST DESIRE… TO BECOME

The desire comes before the 'Be.' The Bible says… "Delight yourself also in the LORD; and He shall give you the Desires of your heart." Psalms 37:4

We as Christians disappoint ourselves because we don't fully understand the scriptures. We must read the preface; the condition of the scripture to qualify for its treasures. The reason why we haven't received the things we've been quoting by the scriptures, is we haven't met the conditions to release them.

Before the promise, there's a requirement! We must first meet the requirement for the scripture to apply to us. God's word works regardless; but we must align ourselves with its requirements to profit from its promises.

MY NAME IS LOVE

So many of us have misinterpreted the Psalms 37 scripture. We automatically thought it, and all scriptures, applied to us. They don't! We must meet their requirements to release them. This scripture requires that we "Delight ourselves in the Lord first, in order for God to give us "The desires of our hearts."

What does this mean? It means we're not just saying we're a Christian. We have a committed relationship with Christ, and our lifestyles bear evidence of it by the fruit of the Spirit.

What are these fruits of the Spirit? The Bible tells us in Galatians 5:22-23… "But the fruit of the Spirit is love, joy, peace, patience, kindness, goodness, faithfulness, gentleness and self-control. Against such things there is no law." We garner these qualities in our life by surrendering our lives to Christ. This means giving up our lives to gain them. This means laying down our desires; to receive the desires of Christ, for our life and purpose.

This brings us to the second part of that scripture… The desires of our heart. This is the part we misinterpret. We believe this scripture tells us that God will give us anything we ask for. That's not what it says. It says He will give us the desires of our Heart, when we delight ourselves in Him. This means when we obey Him, and follow His leadings for our lives.

Let me explain what this looks like. As a Christian for many years, I've also misinterpreted this scripture. I asked God for bright, shiny and new things all the time; only to be disappointed. It's not that I didn't receive some things through the grace of God, and my efforts. I didn't come close to getting what I asked of God. Why?

I may have been a Christian, but I wasn't where I am today… With my life sold out to God. Therefore, my desire back then were for things; material things. I wanted houses, cars and clothes, and that's what I

A WILLINGNESS TO CHANGE

prayed for. It wasn't that God didn't want to give me those things. It's that He didn't want to give me just those things… He wanted me to have it all; the physical and the spiritual. But I had to let go. I had to make room in my heart to receive Him first, before the material. When I did this, God filled my heart with His desires.

This means God will physically/spiritually, place His desires in our hearts. He gives us those things to want, and we now desire them. He replaces our desires with His. These new desires will line up with purpose instead of things.

Before the material things, God wanted me to have Him. He didn't want me just to recognize Him, or just to know about Him. He wanted me to know Him! To know Him like this, I had to surrender my life completely to Him.

My life is no longer about myself. With this, something happened! My desires changed. Did I still want those nice things in life. Sure I did! But they were no longer my priorities.

There was an exchange when I surrendered my life completely to God. Now I desired those things He wanted me to have; those things He wanted to give me. The things I now desired most, were not things… They were Tools!

What were these tools I now greatly desired of God more than trinkets. I desired the Anointing of God; to equip me to minister in the lives of people… To Impact, to Influence, and to Inspire.

We as Christians also misinterpret the Anointing of God. We think it makes us holy, and we fall out on the floor and stuff. No! The anointing are tools to equip us for the service of God. These tools allow us to do what we use to do ordinary; we now do great. It causes others to see the gifts of God at work in our lives.

MY NAME IS LOVE

My greatest desires through surrender was to know, and to walk in my purpose from God. I desired to build His Kingdom, by changing lives and leading them to Christ. I desired to draw people of all ages to the love of God within me.

I now desired those things God placed in my heart. These things were for people; their lives, and their souls. This is what the Psalms scripture means. It means there'll be an exchange in our desires for the things of God. We align our lives with His will and His purpose for our life; and others.

I've never experienced such joy in my life. Surrendering to God didn't ruin my life. It placed me on my path to purpose, and effecting lives for the Kingdom of God. It's where I began to see the work of God effecting the lives of others through me. It's a beautiful thing to see. It's my hearts greatest desire; to be used of God in my purpose, to touch the lives of others.

Surrender is a scary word. It brings with it fears of falling without a net. God catches us when we surrender… In His loving arms!

Our lives change through our desires. The desire comes first… Before the 'Be!" We'll now desire the things and tools of God to equip us for our purpose.

How will we know if our lives are surrendered to God… Just look at the things we desire and they'll tell us where we're at with Him. Do we desire trinkets, or tools. Are we asking God for purses or purpose! Are we asking Him for Saks Fifth Avenue, or for souls! This identifies where we are in Him!

When we trade our desires for God's through our surrender… This is where we truly begin to live life as He intended!

A WILLINGNESS TO CHANGE

TAKING CAPTIVE EVERY THOUGHT

What I'm seeing through the writings God gives me, is that He's not only telling us how to live… He teaching us.

Through marriage, God established the family. Society is the product of the family. It would only stand to reason that we must produce good and stable through our families to effect our society for good. God designed society to all come through His institution of marriage. This gives us a deeper awareness of the importance of our marriages, and how each one of them effects society for good or adversely.

Our marriages and families are the primary target of the enemy. What God loves; he hates. So he would seek to make a mockery of us through our marriages and families; reaping destruction and havoc. The sad part is… We've let him do it; unaware!

As husbands, we must cover our marriages, our spouses, our children with the impenetrable blood of Christ. We must do this through prayer, as the high priest of our homes. We can no longer afford to naively believe that the enemy doesn't seek to kill, steal and destroy in our lives; through our marriages and families. He steals from us through ignorance; by not being aware of what he's doing. He destroys by our lack of gratitude, appreciation and contentment for the blessings God has given us through marriage. This then turns us against each other… And destroys us!

We searched and searched. We cried out to God for a spouse. Years later, we're crying again through complaints, because we've failed to nourish what God has given us.

We expected the marriage to perform on its own, so we put little effort into it. We grew comfortable and complacent. We kicked our shoes off and said, 'I have them now, I can relax!' We let our minds tell us…

MY NAME IS LOVE

'I don't have to do all that stuff I did to attract them before we got married!' You lied! You're wrong!

This is the beginning of ignorance through deceit in your marriage. The truth is… What you did; who you were to attract and get that man or woman, you must do and be, that and more to keep them. Contrary to popular belief… There's no 'Let down' in marriage!

Through whose eyes do you look at your spouse… Yours or God's! This is the problem here… We take the shine off of the armor. We let it get dull. The shine is covered over with the rust of complacency, ill contentment and lack of gratitude. Ladies, you must get the Never Dull out, and start shining that armor by seeing your husband as you once did. Even if he's not, tell your mind these things, and your perspective and image of him will change. This will lead to your beliefs and desires; which will also begin to change your behavior towards him.

Men; you must see that woman as a precious gift from God. Just as you are prince; she is princess, and should be looked at, treated and cherished as such. You too must examine your 'let down,' and change the thoughts in your mind back towards appreciation and gratitude for being blessed to have her. She passed over many to choose you. You pursued her! You were her choice! You were hired for the job of her love and care. You sealed that covenant before God through marriage.

How have we strayed so far! How have we derailed and gotten off track! How have we taken lightly, and for granted. How have we abused through our words or neglect; what we once desired so much!

The answers are many; the solutions few. The Bible tells us how to prevent this from ever happening in our lives and marriages again. It says… "We demolish arguments and every pretension that sets itself up against the knowledge of God, and we take captive every thought to make it obedient to Christ." 2 Corinthians 10:5 We have gotten to

A WILLINGNESS TO CHANGE

this place on our own accord. We're simply products of our thoughts. The Bible also says... "Out of the abundance of the heart, the mouth speaks." Luke 6:25

In our ignorance and neglect; we have not put the right thoughts into our hearts, and have allowed toxic out of our mouths. We have spewed venom on to our spouses. Because our hearts weren't clean, we spilled the residue of them over to the person in physical, emotional and spiritual proximity to us... Our husband; our wife!

This must stop today; not yesterday or tomorrow! The damage has been done. Just look at our society today. Look at the broken homes; the damaged children through our selfish choices of divorce. We've wreaked havoc on society, and wondered why the world looks as it does.

We as Christians have been called to be light to a world in darkness. We've not been! We've gone along ignorant of our responsibilities to the world. The world apart from Jesus, doesn't know what's right for them. After reading what God has given us here... None of us are no longer without excuse!

We must take our place in our marriages, in our homes; in society. We lead through our examples, and the light of Christ within us. The problem being; our lights are dim, or nonexistent to the world crying out for help and guidance. How will they know Christ unless they are shown through us! Someone modeled Him to lead us. We must be the same to the world, through the light of our lives and marriages.

How do we begin to do this? Just as the Bible tells us... First we "Demolish arguments and every pretension that sets itself up against the knowledge of God." What does this mean? It means that everything that stands, criticizes; every gossip, or ungodly friend that attempts through poor advice, or any other means... To disrupt, ruin, come between, or destroy our marriage. It Must be destroyed or put aside!

MY NAME IS LOVE

The Bible instructs us… "Not to walk in the council of the ungodly; nor stand in their ways." Psalms 1:1

Secondly, all of those free thoughts we've had that allowed our minds to stray towards negativity, neglect, lack of gratitude and appreciation, and abuse towards ours spouses; we must take captive every thought we have, and line it up with obedience to Christ.

How do we do this? We must be aware that our minds can produce thoughts to us Unsolicited! Or in other words; without us asking for them. We sit back and wonder where these thoughts came from. It's from our sin nature, that must constantly be checked and regulated.

But you say… 'I'm saved!' Salvation didn't remove your sin nature. The Bible says we still have to "Work out our salvation with fear and trembling." Philippians 2:12 When we get these negative thoughts about our spouse; we must dismiss them, and replace them with positive and productive thoughts. We must train our minds to do this. For all of our lives, we've let our minds tell us what it wanted to. Now that we're in Christ; we must stand at the helm of our thoughts and filter them! The good ones we leave, and act upon. The bad ones we discard.

This wisdom places us on our paths to light and salt producing marriages as God intended. This wisdom used, can restore the romance, the spark; the fire in our marriages. Instead of the negativity our minds tell us… We give our minds good thoughts, and these good thoughts produce our outlooks and behaviors.

Don't allow any of your thoughts to run loose! Take them captive, and line them up to the obedience of Christ. We'll then begin to live, and walk in the success God ordained for us in our marriages, and all other aspects of our lives!

A WILLINGNESS TO CHANGE

TIME CAUGHT UP

They weren't for then. They were for now. For such a time as this.

I couldn't imagine wearing those shoes I bought. They sat brand new in my closet for years untouched. I looked at them at times and even wondered why I purchased them. God knew why! Now they're the ones I wear the most! Time has caught up with their purpose! It's their time!

When time and reason caught up with the purpose of Joseph, in one day; one moment, he went from prisoner to Governor over all Egypt. He became second in command to Pharaoh, in what looked like an instant. It wasn't! His time had reached his season over time.

When God tells us it's our season, that season is attached to a time. They'll be a time before the season starts. The season is connected to our purpose. It's the place we walk in it fully.

In between was his preparation, and his training. His suffering stripped him of his pride, and gave him the gift of humility. His pain robbed him of his anger, and gave him the gift of forgiveness for what his brothers did to him. His suffering gave him the gifts of insight, awareness and wisdom; as he looked back upon it. He could see the Hand of God directing him to greatness... Not to his punishment!

It was God that orchestrated, or allowed the pit, the betrayal and the prison. Which tells us that even what man tries to do to us, falls within the Sovereignty, the parameters and the plans and purpose of God. It was a placement, not a punishment; that would lead to the greatest promotion on Earth. Time had caught up with the purpose of Joseph. What may have looked like one day, was years in the making; giving him the humility and character to walk in his office with excellence!

MY NAME IS LOVE

We may have a season to walk in from God. But that season has a time before its ever released by God to us, and for us. In the interim, God prepares us with the gifts we need to walk in our office with excellence. Gifts such as humility, compassion, love, care, concern for others, wisdom, awareness, clarity, sobriety and others. How do we obtain these precious gifts?Most often we obtain them through failure, hardships, betrayals… Through suffering!

So we must learn as James said to "Count it all joy when we fall into various temptations, knowing that the trying of our faith works patience. And let patience have its turn, that you may be perfect and compete; lacking nothing." James 1:2-4 It's the trials and suffering that prepares us for the greatness God has for us. We don't get the skills we need to fulfill our character without them.

The greatest lesson are built in pain. These are the lessons we remember, the ones we never take for granted; the ones that become most dear to us. We learn from them quickly, and never seek to venture back into those areas through foolishness. It's getting burnt on the stove. We don't go back to it! They stay at home with us; close to our hearts and minds. They're kept promptly in the section called… Do Not Repeat! Pain attached! Pain teaches us quick, valuable and lasting lessons. It obtains our full attention. We surrender our pride in exchange for wisdom. It takes us to places success never could. As a matter of fact, it will be the reason for our success. Pain is the preparation of God for His plans & purpose over our lives.

We must learn to see with truth and awareness that it's not the punishment of God… It's the preparation of God through pain that equips us for the office of our purpose; to walk in it with excellence and humility, before a world filled with pride and arrogance. This is when, where and how, we become light and salt. Light to illuminate the way. A compass to point to the path. Salt for a world to desire and thirst for

A WILLINGNESS TO CHANGE

the change of character they've seen in us through the transformation of God in our lives.

Lord, may we see the Purpose in our pain.

BAD PEOPLE RUIN US FOR THE RIGHT ONE

The one thing we don't think of relationships for is... Purpose! We think of them for romance, a cure for loneliness; togetherness, but not for purpose.

It's one of the most important decisions we'll ever make in life... Who we connect ourselves and partner with. This can propel us in life, or set us back substantially. It can help us to walk in our purpose from God. It can cause us to wander in the wilderness; going in circles for years, as the Israelites did for their poor decisions and disobedience.

When will we wake up to this truth... That bad relationships are no good for us. They set us back! They rob and steal precious time we can't recover. They leave us emotionally down hill trying to get back up. They bankrupt our hearts; leaving us emotionally cold and callous for the right one God would send to us. When they appear, we're physically and mentally spent; to accept and recognize the good God brings us... To connect us back to our path called purpose.

They leave us emotionally bankrupt!
Too many withdrawals... Too few deposits!

We become emotional skeletons of ourselves. We come across hard and withholding; unavailable for expression, other than raw and harsh words. You may think you give out emotionally... But how much do you withhold! You've become a fortress; rather than a castle!

MY NAME IS LOVE

We should be fortresses for wrong people, and castles for the right one God sends. You will never live in a castle with a bad man or woman in your life. They'll distract you from God's true purpose for your life. You'll live in constant drama and foolishness, instead of moving forward in life and marriage.

God calls us all to be light and salt to the world. These kind of relationships leave us never igniting our lights, nor producing salt. We can't go anywhere, for the drama in our homes; due to the relationships we choose.

We must ask ourselves of anyone that approaches us these and many other questions… What are this person's motives? What do they really want from me? Do they only want a physical relationship with me? What are their goals in life? Where are they headed? How do they feel about God? Are they saved? Have they been filled with the Holy Spirit? What do you think of a woman? Is she your partner in life and purpose, or your maid and house keeper?

The world cares nothing about our lives, our purpose, our bodies; other than what they can extract from us. Then they leave us barren and wounded; hoping we can recover for who's right for us.

We can no longer use this algorithm or equation in something as important as a relationship; where we become spiritually one entity with another person. We can't afford to in this world of chaos, selfishness and confusion. We must align our choices with prayer. We must connect our decisions with wisdom. We must seek God for our life partner; rather than to be led by our flesh.

For the first time in our lives, we must look beyond looks, as the sole factor in our selection process. Yes, attraction draws us to the person; but only substance can keep us there.

A WILLINGNESS TO CHANGE

Substance such as… Do they have a personal relationship with Christ! These days, don't take their word for it. Examine their fruit by their actions towards you, life and others. You can't afford to be blind any longer!

Look how they interact with others. Look how they are when they're angry. Do they fight fair. Do they pout, or apologize afterwards. Are they peaceful, or a fire starter. Do they always have some drama and confusion around them. Look how responsible, or irresponsible they are with their finances. Could I follow this person where they're leading me; or will their lifestyle go beyond my beliefs and convictions.

We must know… We must know!

The best and most successful reason to partner with someone, is for you to join each other in the purpose of God over your lives. This is the magic we leave out of the equation; in our search for love.

You want to find the deepest, purest, rarest kind of love, that each day you walk in fullness of life… Partner with the person God sends you; not the one your flesh finds you. You can do incredible things partnered with the right person in life. You can accomplish amazing things together.

None of us truly live outside of our purpose from God. Yes, we go through life, and we even exist. But I'm talking about truly living! This kind of living takes us to

an entirely different stratosphere. It's a life where two join together, to live out their purpose of God assigned to affect life, living and society.

Weigh your decisions carefully. Open your eyes fully to see. Observe the flags and the fruit! Gather the fruit. Move away from the flags.

MY NAME IS LOVE

You must ask… Does this person connect me to my purpose; or remove me farther from it! God, life and the world are dependent upon you to make the right decision. Don't make it for flesh. Make it for purpose! You'll experience life in an entirely new direction.

Chapter 12

OUR PRIDE MUST GO

~ We don't add one thing to God. He's Absolute and All Efficient on His own! ~

WHEN PEOPLE WANT TO INVEST IN YOUR LIFE

When people want to invest in your life… Let them! This was a lesson I had to learn. It's hard for me to ask anyone for anything. Maybe that's an area of my pride that I need to work on. But I try not to burden people. I'm normally the one wanting to help others.

But I've had to learn, to put my pride aside because I was standing in the way of others being blessed. God has brought some incredible people in my life to support me in the things I do for others. Through The Aubrey Stewart Project, we have a scholarship for a male and female for 10 years now. We have a Jr. Ambassador Award for 8th Graders, for eight years. We have a program for little boys and little girls without Dads in their lives. We honor and recognize people in the community making amazing contributions through The Aubrey Stewart Award for Excellence.

When people see you doing good for others, they want to be a part of it. I have many special men in my life, but Mr. Pat Masón taught me a valuable lesson recently.

MY NAME IS LOVE

Mr. Mason is a wonderful man. He's kind, generous and humble. On many occasions, Mr. Mason has called me and informed me that he had something to give me. We would always meet at our same place… The old Pizza Hut parking lot.

This time was different. In his giving, Mr. Mason would impart a valuable lesson in my life. As always, he was being his generous self. This time he wanted to purchase some Tuskegee Airmen coins and give them to me to give to our scholarship winners and other students we recognize.

Here came the hard part! Mr. Mason says… "What are we looking at here; do we want to get a role of ten or twenty coins." I love Mr. Mason, and it's hard for me to take anything from him. But this wasn't about me. This was about him being blessed, and I had to move out of the way for him to receive it.

I said… Mr. Mason, I can purchase the coins, if you give me the information. Here then came the words that would change my pride into accepting from others. This is what Mr. Mason said… "You have to let me do this! It makes me feel a part of what you're doing!" It nearly brought tears to my eyes.

Mr. Mason sees my efforts in trying to do good for others, and he wanted to do anything he could to feel apart of what God was doing in the lives of others. I told him thank you, and for teaching me a tremendous lesson on receiving.

So many of us give; but it's just as important to receive what others invest in our lives. Their giving is connected to a blessing, as they are now the giver to the giver. If you're a giver; it's humbling, but it's an important lesson to learn.

OUR PRIDE MUST GO

Thank you Mr. Pat Mason, and to all the incredible people that God has brought into my life, on my mission to do for others. In the service of God; we must be both givers; and receivers!

It's a beautiful thing to give... But sometimes; the giver has to receive too!

He's such a humble man; he didn't even want me to mention his name in this writing!

Sorry Mr. Mason... I want All of the world to know about you!

> "TJ you're a blessing, you have the ability and the capacity to pull that out of others; to pull out in me things I want to do for others!"

Mr. Pat Mason

I'M NOT ATTACKING... I'M PROBLEM SOLVING

The defensive will never receive help. They have removed all internal mirrors within; or covered their reflection. The problem always lies within someone else; their theme.

None of us are perfect. I've always admired those who could laugh at themselves. Those who never took themselves so seriously. People like my favorite actor, Mr. Cary Grant. Smooth, suave, handsome; he wasn't too cool to be silly. He had the confidence to laugh at himself. He had the strength to allow us to laugh at him. It took nothing from who he was, yet broadened him as a gentleman, an actor and respected human being. His, was a rare quality.

His internal mirror gave him room to be class personified; yet beloved actor that made us laugh in his handsomeness. So many of us can't

MY NAME IS LOVE

be both. We don't know how to be. He did it with ease and it did not detract one iota from the respect and admiration we had for him. As a matter of fact, it only endeared us to him, as it made us see how one who was at the pinnacle of his profession and a standard of class, didn't take himself too seriously to also make us laugh. Somehow this brought him on our level where we could touch him with our lives.

Seeing this, allowed me to translate how many of us are in life and relationships. We see ourselves one way. The internal mirror of our heart is small and linear, rather than large and encompassing. This gives us little room to see ourselves as anything or anyone else. And when others notice the cracks in our armor; we lash out rather than look deeper within.

Our perspectives are narrow. We see ourselves, life and the world; as leading actors, never in need of an acting coach or further education. The skilled continues practicing his craft lifelong, as a physician practices medicine; never fully mastered. He leaves room for growth through constructive and even destructive criticism. Each instance, he returns to his internal mirror; wide and broad, noticing the chinks in his armor he must repair.

The over sensitive, over confident, self promoting; never find this place and time within. They medicate with the balm of vanity, rather than introspective healing and reconditioning.

We often find such a one argumentative, loud, reclusive or evasive. The outlook from their portal... The problem is the world; not me!

But change we all must do. Dust off and enlarge the internal mirrors of our hearts and minds to reflect our image; ever expansive; large and in constant need of tuning.

These are the beautiful ones, with an healthy sense of self; never deprecating, but knowing in life; all things must change. Even us, the best and the worst of us must ever evolve and succumb to the criticism of our hearts and others. For only in this we learn, we grow; we expand our depth and range in life to become illuminating to others.

We must accept the words of others; the darts and the flares, and find if any truth within. For even the darts and the arrows with flames bring light to shine on our internal mirrors; to find us lacking and incomplete.

Only the wise finds reward in this; as a man who finds great treasure. For he can see what may have been sent to hurt, harm or injure… Actually gave him light and space to adjust and enlarge the internal mirror of his heart; producing character. This did not quench his light within; yet only broadened… To make him more illuminating and attractive to others; to see.

THE LOUDNESS OF SILENCE

It woke me up out of a sound sleep. It wasn't the disturbance of noise… .It was silence!

It's one of the most beautiful things you find in the discovery of your purpose… The absence of Pride!

What do I mean by that. Pride prevents us from doing and being many things. It's prevents us from expressing our true feelings and emotions about life and others. So we keep it all locked in a vault inside of us.

The difference I've found when discovering your purpose from God and life is… You unlock those treasures within your heart and distribute them as they were intended.

MY NAME IS LOVE

Life today works in opposites. Pride tells us it's lowly and beneath us to be servants of one another. That couldn't be farther from the truth. It was through my job in the Air Force, meeting the needs of VIP's that I learned the true definition of service.

Service is a beautiful thing. It's a pleasure to be a servant. Service and our gifts go together; hand in hand. There's no one without the other. It's meeting the needs of others through the absence of pride. This absence of Pride could simply see something good in someone; a child, a teenager, and encourage them on their path. This absence of Pride could also be a confession; because real life isn't about us... It's about the lives we touch with ours!

I got injured while in the Air Force. Nothing serious, but years later on my job at the Department of Labor, my duties changed and so did my dormant injuries. In just three years I would go from 30% disabled to 100%, with horrible pain to accompany the injuries; non stop for the last 18 years.

Many times, I thought about taking my life as a means to escape the pain. Why am I telling you this? Not to feel sorry for me; but to prove something!

Unless you knew me, you wouldn't even know I was disabled and in terrible pain in your presence. It's not that I hide it! Your presence is more important to me; and I don't let it distract me.

People see me doing many things in the community for children, adults and anyone I can recognize. This pain hasn't stopped me from doing this. I have the desire to serve others in spite of the pain.

But as I sleep, I must have noise to distract my mind; to somewhat shut it down to rest. Constant thoughts of my mind telling me I hurt, is combatted by the noise of a comedy on TV.

Early this morning, the battery on my phone died. The comedy that had silenced my mind went off with the phone. I awoke immediately; from the soundness of my sleep... To the loudness of Silence!

My point is this... Do I always feel like doing the things I do for others? I desire to, and it outweighs the pain. The day you discover your purpose and that moment you toss aside your pride and realize the beauty of being a servant; are the days you truly begin to live.

The secret of life is easy... Life isn't about us; but only as we connect our lives in service to others!

Do I like living in pain every day of my life. Not at all! But it was the pain which directed me to my purpose.

For the lives I'm privileged to be a part of... I'll silence my mind with service to others!

THE PRIVILEGE OF YOU

Out of billions... You we're the one. Beside me as I sleep and in life... I appreciate you.

There's so much in life we take for granted. Some of us have been blessed to find our life partner; that one person out of millions we would love enough to join our lives together in matrimony. Such elation at first. Then the routine of life, of work, of responsibilities kicks in. We allow the routine, and do nothing to modify it. We settle. We get complacent. We allow in dullness; rather than spice.

We look to the world for excitement, rather than to God for wisdom and direction to alter our hearts, lives and marriage. We start to complain rather than to seek answers through prayer together.

MY NAME IS LOVE

We lose focus. Get distracted. Now we find ourselves in the land of lack of gratitude, which puts us in the land of ill contentment; which causes us to desires greener grasses.

We've been tricked, fooled and deceived. Our selfish hearts have now removed us out of purpose; and our flesh has taken the helm of our lives. Blindly we go; with destruction in our wake. We search for what we already had.

Do you not know that the Bible says... "The thief comes only to steal and kill and destroy. I came that they may have life and have it abundantly." John 10:10 Anyone; including your own flesh and selfish nature, who would seek to remove you from your marriage is a thief. Don't be deceived; your own flesh will rob and steal from you if you don't constantly keep it submitted to the Spirit of God within you. Yes, there's a real enemy out there who desires to kill and destroy you. But he would only want to kill you if you're a threat to him by serving God and walking in your purpose; effecting lives for the Kingdom of God.

Otherwise, he just wants to kill and destroy what you have. To him you are of great use. In your destruction you can be used to take out yourself and those around you. Those you're connected to like your husband and children; your marriage. With you dead, you're of no use to him. But alive; selfish and your flesh at the helm of your life... You're destructive!

As your flesh sought greener pastures and you've left destruction in your wake; now you look back in emptiness and desire what God once gave you. You had it all and was led astray! If you have a desire for greener pastures; it wasn't from God. It was the world and it's enticements. God does not move us to greener pastures. He requires that we water and fertilize our own with love, care and attention. God's desire is that you prosper in your own marriage, where you've been placed, to effect the lives of your spouse, children and others.

OUR PRIDE MUST GO

If you didn't know it; now you do. It's not the devil thats you're biggest enemy. It's someone much closer to you… It's your Flesh!

WE PUSH AWAY THE RIGHT

How can we want what's bad for us; who's bad for us, and push away the good! What's so attractive about bad, and not attractive about good! That makes no sense! It's our minds and images that must be changed. It's our images that must be aligned and renewed with truth; no longer deceit and foolishness.

What can you expect from a shark; an alligator, except to get bitten or worse! The Bible tells us… "Can a man take fire into his blossom and not be burned!" Proverbs 6:27 What this is saying to us in the natural world of our lives today is… Do you expect to bring and allow bad into your life and believe it's not going to negatively affect you, your plans, your purpose; your destiny! Maybe you don't have plans and that's the problem. Maybe you don't have a path, and your focus is misaligned.

Who ever told us we could fix another individual! Change is made in the heart of a man and only God can construct a change in us. Anything else is only temporary at best; for the sake of silence, or getting us what we want.

Look back at the pattern in your life! You've been expecting something good from what you already knew as bad. That's called foolishness! The fruit is in the tree. It can produce its own fruit.

What makes us think we can change a grown human being with a mind and will of their own. The most we can do is manipulate them into a temporary agreement; that reverts back to the original character once the fussing and the smoke has cleared.

MY NAME IS LOVE

We must learn! Apple trees will only give us apples. Thorn bushes will only give us thorns!

We push away the apples to embrace the thorns!

WE HAVE WRONGLY DESCRIBED AND SEEN STRENGTH

There's no strength in meanness! I often hear people express to others and to the world... How strong they are!

I've heard it so many times... I'm a strong... !!! The truth is; we only tell out loud what we're trying to convince ourselves and others what we are. And we speak it loud too so everyone can hear us. This is not a declaration of truth... But most often a Cry for Help!

We tell ourselves in silence; who we truly are! No need to shout! Only words whispered to our conscious and subconscious minds producing character which shows up in our lives as fruit! The tree doesn't scream or shout to produce it's fruit... It does it in silence and evidence! True beauty doesn't proclaim it... It just is; no words need be spoken! The mountain doesn't proclaim its heights. The sea doesn't shout of its depths... They simply are; in their magnificence!

Life and the world know who and what we are by our character, not just what we profess and proclaim. We're not always what we speak!

And I'm sure in most cases, the word strength when used to define us; is misaligned and misinterpreted.

There's no strength in being mean, loud, boisterous, aggressive; violent. These behaviors describe the absence of strength because they all lack self control of our minds, mouths and bodies!

OUR PRIDE MUST GO

Strength is never partnered with an absence of self control. We have misinterpreted and wrongly defined the true meaning and characteristics of strength, which according to the Bible are... Love, Joy, Peace, Patience, Kindness, Goodness, Gentleness, Faithfulness, & Self-Control.

When we walk in these fruits we exhibit strength. Telling someone off, being aggressive, being loud, boisterous are all an absence of strength. We can tell the world what we believe we are... But the Bible tells us the truth about ourselves.

There is no strength in the lack of self control of our minds, mouths and bodies! Strength is control, restraint and resistance!

PERSPECTIVE

My car wouldn't start when I took it in for an inspection. It turns out that the belt on the alternator broke.

How do you look at things? To me, I saw this as a blessing. The blessing was not that my car broke, but it broke where I was safe. I wasn't on the freeway stranded and I was at a mechanic's garage.

The same day, I drove my car to the car wash. Water got inside the car and it stalled. I had to push it out of the car wash, and into a parking spot. The car got real heavy on an incline and I had to put the emergency brake on, as it was as far as I could push it.

A man in a truck stopped behind me. He saw me struggling. He got out of his truck and came towards me. He was assisted by crutches and had only one leg. This man got behind my car and helped me push it into the parking spot.

MY NAME IS LOVE

With joy and astonishment, I rushed to shake his hand, and tell him how much I appreciated him.

Sometimes, when things go wrong, our first response is to complain. I try to see things through the eyes of gratitude.

It's a beautiful world… It all depends on how you look at it!

REACHING IS VULNERABILITY

Reaching is vulnerability. Reaching is exposure; the exposure of heart and soul. Reaching is leaning towards, making effort to connect; to touch.

Yet it leaves our hearts exposed, wide open to hurt; rejection. Reaching is taking the first steps, when no one is moving. Reaching is making intentions known, aware; clear.

Reaching is uncertainty; not necessarily reciprocation. Reaching is tremendous strength, never weakness.

For merely a moment, I've felt and described a fraction of what God feels constantly… Reaching, vulnerable, exposing His heart to the heartless, blind, unaware; rejecting Him!

It's equivalent to the rejection from a child you've given birth to, loved and given your all and very best to, and yet they've turned their back on you; rejecting your every attempt at love.

Yet He still continues; constantly and unending.

Yet He continues!

OUR PRIDE MUST GO

COMPETE ONLY WITH YOURSELF

What God has for you is for you. God has an Infinite amount of All things. His supply is not diminished by giving to you or your neighbor. Therefore, there's no need for jealousy, envy, backbiting, strife, or any such thing. Focus only on what God has for you; not your neighbor.

Rejoice in the success of others! Be their biggest cheerleaders! This is a sign of your growth and maturity.

You've realized, you've believed in the Unlimited of God. You've realized that what He's done for others, He can do differently and even greater for you. And most importantly, you now understand; what others have… NEVER DIMINISHES the Vast, Boundless, Unlimited resources of God.

HAD HE NOT LEFT

Had Maurice White not left The Ramsey Lewis Trio as a drummer, there would be no Earth Wind & Fire. Look at all of the beautiful music that would not have been created.

It's that pull, that tug that tells us we are no longer comfortable where we are; who we are. We want more! It's that tug of destiny pulling us towards our purpose in life!

It's that uneasiness. It's that, wanting to branch out; lengthen your wings, gather them and soar. It's wanting to go places others can't see or imagine. Because you've seen yourself already there. You're trying to go there; to that place. Your heart is trying to take you there! Don't ignore it! Move towards its leading, guidance and directions. Don't discount anything! Small steps are all part of a larger plan and picture, which we seldom see until we've looked back from where we've come.

MY NAME IS LOVE

It's the desire God placed within us to be unique; different... Special! Few take the journey. Many bask on the shores of contentment. This requires an ocean voyage, away from the safe waters of the shore.

To see the grand and magnificent, you must move towards it. You must go where it leads. You must follow its direction.

There's wisdom that far surpasses our own out there. There's so much more to life and the world. I want to walk in these places. I want to be these things. The greatness I see in others, I want to surpass; being grateful for its leading and enlightenment.

CHASING GHOSTS

Real or imagined, empty, hollow; unclothed in substance; lacking presence here or there. An illusion. A figment of reality. False intentions. A perception of real. Slightly involved, not devoted or committed to togetherness; to forever. Self seeking, self involved... Others lacking.

It's fruitless Chasing Ghost!

SAUL WAS ONCE ANOINTED OF GOD

Emotions don't make us spiritual. In these times, we have got to get back to the church being the one place we find truth. We have gone astray and have followed man, rather than truth. Truth alone is found only in and through one source... The word of God!

We have missed the mark. We have misinterpreted. We have walked in wrong beliefs. We have adopted our own doctrines based on our opinions, rather than truth.

OUR PRIDE MUST GO

We have believed that emotions make us spiritual. We believed that the anointing makes us holy. We have misinterpreted and walked misaligned with truth.

The church environment is not a true litmus test of who we really are. The rest of the week days are more inline with the truth of who we are. We come to church already hyped up, pumped up on who we're going to be. How is it that we're this person on Sunday; and a different person the rest of the week!

The church must once again be a lighthouse to the world. None of us are perfect, but we should at least resemble the people we proclaim to be. The Bible tells us… "Wherefore by their fruits you shall know them." Matthew 7:10 It's not our words that bare witness to the truth of who we are; it's our fruits, or lack of them which does.

We have confused dancing, running around the church as spiritual; rather than emotions. It's not that those things are not a part of our spirituality. Being spiritual is living from that place within us where our spirit man yields to The Holy Spirit within us. And this is for the most part, the basis of our decisions, choices and lifestyles. It doesn't mean that we walk around with our heads in the clouds, it means we're grounded in truth.

We have also confused being anointed of God with being holy. Again, we think this causes us to be, and act a certain way at church. God once said this truth to me… "Why are people only anointed at church!" The truth is, the anointing of God are tools bestowed upon us to equip us to do the work and purpose of God assigned to our lives. This doesn't make us holy. Living a life set apart for God, absent from the world makes us holy. It also gives us humility. The closer we live to God, the more humble we should be.

MY NAME IS LOVE

Saul was once anointed by God. He was the first king of Israel. He was anointed to do a job; to govern the people of God. He did everything but. Due to his disobedience, he was rejected by God. He didn't display spirituality or humility. He displayed jealousy, resentment, envy and he tried to kill David, whom God anointed to eventually replace him as king of Israel.

Being anointed didn't make Saul holy, spiritual or cause him to bear fruit… His obedience, his choices, his decisions and his lifestyle were the only things that could have done that.

We can learn from Saul. Yes we're anointed of God, but that's only the beginning of where we start. The anointing of God gives us the ability to do something ordinary; extraordinary. But only if we walk in obedience to God. Saul was not the example of being spiritual or holy either. His actions sprung from his own selfish desires and were not motivated by love and compassion; but rather jealousy, envy and seeking to retain his power.

The truth here is this… God gives us things to do and to be in this life. The choice is ours whether we'll pursue them in obedience to him, or never accomplish them; by living from ourselves, rather than the Holy Spirit within us.

The gifts of God don't make us holy… Holiness is our choice to set aside our lives and align them with the desires and will of God for our lives.

FEAR

It's fear… it's the reason we hate, the reason we fight; the reason we're jealous. It all stems from fear!

OUR PRIDE MUST GO

We hate because we're afraid of something or someone. We're afraid so we adopt the mindset of… I'll do to you, before you can do to me!

We fear because we believe what's in my heart is in yours. It's believing a perception rather than a reality. It's the cause of most of the world's problems.

Jealousy comes with suspicion. It's our fear of losing someone, or someone having more than us. In it, we surrender our peace of mind and emotions.

Fear encapsulates our hearts; keeps it rigid and unyielding. It blocks our hearts, rather than keeping them receptive and flowing. It blinds us to avenues and ideas. It seeks firmness rather than fluidity. It robs us of solutions. We seek to ensnare and capture, rather than to release and free.

Due to fear, we seek to control others. We want them only where we feel safe. We box them in. We give them no room; no freedom for expression.

Give us only what we want! Take me not from the safety of my prison! Don't move me or cause me to change, stretch my heart, mind or imagination. Leave me in the confines of my safety, where I'm free to flounder in mediocrity and non-advancement.

Fear cripples! Fear placed in others pushes them away; keeps them from being close. We hold at a distance, rather than closely. We miss out!

Jealousy is the fear of loss; of replacement. Hate is the fear of love. Contention; arguing, is the fear of peace.

What are we afraid of? Are we afraid of fear? Are we afraid of change? Do we lack courage? Are we afraid of the unknown? Are we afraid of

MY NAME IS LOVE

understanding? Are we afraid of others opinions of us? Are we afraid of aggression? Are we afraid of losing our place, status or perception?

Fear is a protective mechanism in the body to alert us to immediate or present danger. Fear is healthy in a response or a reaction, but it's an unhealthy and dangerous place to live in. It's an unwise place to make long term decisions. Fear can slide us into hate. Fear is a place to warn us; not a place to stay!

After Joseph became Governor of all of Egypt, he brought his family to live close to him. The promise of God to his great grandfather Abraham, was that He would multiply his seed as numerous as the stars.

This didn't happen in Abraham's life, nor did it happen in Isaac's time. The fulfillment of this prophecy came through the prosperity and the success of Joseph in Egypt.

It was when Joseph moved his father Jacob to Canaan; they began to increase in vast numbers. After Jacob; Joseph and the pharaoh that promoted Joseph all died. The new pharaoh began to look around and found themselves outnumbered by the offspring of Jacob.

Fear set in. Unwarranted and unnecessary fear set in so much, that pharaoh imagined a untruthful scenario. He imagined because of the number of the Israelites, a people living in peace, would one day take over them as Egyptians; for the sheer size of their population. Their solution! Make slaves of them!

Fear caused the Israelites to live as slaves for 400 years! When we fear, we assume an imaginary situation. We react; rather than respond with wisdom. Fear is a necessary response to protect us in danger. It's not the necessary response to control a people for assumed and imaginary situations.

OUR PRIDE MUST GO

Wisdom, communication; mediation was the greater answer. If God could save these people in their greatest years of famine through the wisdom of one man; Joseph… He could have saved them from making slaves of millions of lives through the wisdom of one man whose decisions weren't predicated on fear!

Fear enslaved millions of lives that could have lived free. We must think of other solutions in life based on wisdom, or we too enslave ourselves and others to fear and foolishness.

Fear is I'll do to you before you do to me. It's I'll hurt you before you hurt me. Are we just afraid of truth. Are we afraid of who we really are… Or who we're really not!

BLAME

Blame… A mechanism of deflection to place fault onto others and neglect to see the problem in ourselves.

Blame is empty; it's fluff! It accomplishes nothing. It solves nothing; it provides no solution, nor moves the situation forward.

With blame, you will end up right where you started! You will find no answer or remedy. One is left feeling no better from hollering; neither having fixed or repaired the problem.

Blame is the opposite of wisdom and responsibility. It seeks to escape, rather than to muster up; and take charge for our shortcomings.

Constructive communication places light on a situation, and gives ample room to discover solutions. This is wisdom, where we discuss; rather than blame. Where we accept responsibility; rather than flee from it. Where we seek what is mutually beneficial; rather than what's self serving. Where we offer apologies, remorse; awareness… And we

MY NAME IS LOVE

move forward having grown and learned; how we can seek not to repeat our offenses and injustices.

Such great strength and wisdom in problem solving together. Such weakness in blame!

AGENDAS… WE ALL HAVE THEM

It's what we want, what we expect from a relationship. It's the unspoken thing we go into a relationship seeking. Sometimes it's revealed. Other times it's hidden.

When our agendas are revealed, it becomes an understanding between two people. It can even become a plan or a goal. The trouble is, when people enter our lives with hidden agendas. They know them but we don't. They have plans and purposes for us other than what they tell us. They hide their true intentions. Their true motive is not to love or remain, but to extract something they need or want from us.

This happens every day in life and relationships. A man approaches a woman, but what is his true agenda. What motivated him to reach out to her. Was it because he was attracted to her; because she had a nice body, she works and he doesn't, she has a place and he needs a place to live, is she the next victim on his list of casualties, or could he find genuine or long term interest from her. A woman must ask all of these questions in her mind or out loud.

This is a spiritual truth that women today must be aware of… The woman serves a vital role in God's plan in society, and she must take her proper place. It was the woman the serpent used in the beginning to destroy man from his originally intended place from God. It's the woman he uses today to keep man confused, distracted and beneath his purpose.

OUR PRIDE MUST GO

These are critical times in our lives. The world is in disarray. Families are broken, and the divorce rate, even for Christian marriages; are higher than ever.

God has established a mandate for change. He's bringing these things to our awareness for us to change, and to get in line with truth. It starts with our relationships. Relationships leads to our families, and our families make up society.

We can't continue on this dangerous path of poor choices and bad decisions in our relationships. It's one of the main ways the enemy robs us of our peace and our focus on God. If you've got a bad relationship, it can affect you spiritually, emotionally, financially, on your job, your relationship with your family; and even with your children.

We must pray for discernment. We must ask God to reveal to us the true intentions of this person. We must be willing to accept the answer He reveals to us, by their behavior; or by their actions. Don't expect God just to tell you. He may; He can do as He pleases. But God also speaks to us through the actions and behaviors of others. It's those things they do that alert us that something's not quite right. It's those signs that make you question their true intentions.

God speaks to us, the problem is; we just don't want to hear what He has to say. The end result is us getting used, hurt, damaged; abused and then we cry out to God... God, why didn't You tell me this person wasn't good for me! He tried to tell you through the signs and subtleties of their behavior, but you wouldn't listen or see the warning signs.

We can not afford another bad relationship. Our children can't afford it either. Look at who we bring around our children; asking them to accept our messes. It's not fair to them. Look at the damage we do to them by our choices. Here you bring someone in your life that wants you, but not your children. This is the warning sign that this isn't the

225

MY NAME IS LOVE

person God has for you. Why would God give you someone who wants you and not your children! He wouldn't; and we need to stop falling for this nonsense.

Let me tell you what God said to a very dear friend of mine. She wanted to be married. She already had two children before marriage. She asked God for a husband. What God said to her I'll never forget. It was the truth so profoundly spoken, and never even thought of by women with children asking God for a husband. This is what God said to her… "You have lost your right to look for a husband. What you need; is a father for your children!" I've never heard such truths about this before!

Women with children look in the wrong places for a husband. They're looking for a man for themselves. If they had children before marriage, God says your search needs to include a man, not just good for you; but for your children also!

We can no longer afford to keep making the same mistakes; walking blindly into relationships, looking for wrong things. If you have children, your agenda has been changed, and now because of your choices; your search will be different, your motives will be different. You now have a different agenda; one which includes searching for a man that will accept and love you and your children.

If you're a man or a woman that don't like kids, then don't even bother with someone with kids. Don't even go down that road of hurting someone or their children if you know this isn't for you… Just because you're attracted to them; they're fine, or you want them sexually. It's a trap! It's one we can't keep putting ourselves into.

Everyone has an agenda. Agendas are not bad; only if they're used incorrectly to hurt, harm, use or to take advantage of. But we each need

OUR PRIDE MUST GO

an agenda. It's a target; a goal we set before us to not go out into the dating world ignorant, but prepared, knowledgeable and ready.

Now that God has defined this important part of a relationship, we must use this wisdom to make better choices for ourselves, our lives and for our children. The Bible tells us this truth... "A person's own folly leads to their ruin, yet their heart rages against the LORD." Proverbs 19:3 The fault is never with God; it's self inflicted!

DECIDE…

THEN BE!

I chose to be a good husband. I simply made a choice to be, and my mind, body, actions and desires manifested towards what I chose!

It's not that complicated. We over analyze things. I asked God to show me how to love my wife. I presented and laid my will at the feet of God. A will He won't violate. A will He won't move upon until asked or surrendered.

Bring it to my attention. I adjust my behavior! We lead with our feelings!

Rather… Lead with your choice; your commitment!

ALLOW ME LORD

YOU'VE BEEN ENDOWED WITH THE HIGHEST OFFICE ON EARTH... SERVANT!

Allow me to show You to the world Lord, in all Your glory and splendor... In love, in beauty; in light. May people see You as they've never seen You before; in truth and understanding. May they see You as the loving Father You are, not a god far off in the distance. But closer than they could ever imagine.

Reach, touch, enlighten to the brightness of Your being Father. Father grant me opportunities for my imagination. Grant me a platform to share and express Your bounty.

THE VOICE OF WISDOM

Speak to me Unlimited. Share with me your bounty. Take me to places unknown and vast. Share with me opportunities, chances of a lifetime; unlimited wealth. Wrap me in Your glory. Set me upon a high stage; that I may do much for many.

Let opportunity be my lifestyle. Let riches and wealth of ideas and ingenuity be my standard. With ease, let me walk through life, as if knowing it's secrets of success and prosperity... Being it's top; it's highest percentage.

MY NAME IS LOVE

I Adore You! Your voice is lovely. Your ways are gentle. Your pursuits are mighty and galant. You come to me as a new day; never seen but embraced.

I marvel at Your magnificence. I am Your offspring. I am identified in others through You. You set me as marvelous and magnificent. I am Your ways; Your voice, Your mannerisms… Your instrument.

Find great delight in me. Shine me upon Your great light. For deep are Your ways. And vast are Your precepts.

I honor You in delight… O Magnificent!

MY PRAYER LORD

DEAR LORD...

Unlock the capacity of my mind; my thoughts to receive much in many ways. That my mind would meld; subconscious dreams with conscious reality. That my thoughts would be a fortress; a vault to hold Your bounty.

Place me Lord where I can excel the most; reach the highest, touch the few & many. Lavish me in love, compassion and care for humanity.

I'm asking for those desires that come to my mind. I'm catching them in my dreams and my imagination. I'm not allowing my creativity to be watered down with the new day.

Partner me in Purpose Lord. Connect me with my dreams and my desires. Clothe me in Excellence. Anoint me to draw, to impact, to lead to You. Gift me in goodness. Supply me with love. Let Your Excellence be seen and heard through me.

Give me the one to see value, worth and purpose in me; through the eyes of appreciation and through the arms of care, gratitude and concern. Let her heart forever be open to love and the receipt of me; that I may know no lack in my life. Let me be her answer, her prayer for that place that only You held for me to fill. That one who will assist me in doing good for others. That it would no longer be a chore to receive love. But I would receive

MY NAME IS LOVE

it in abundance. That I would see the person of You in love Lord through this individual. Whose light will forever shine in homes, relationships and in marriages. That she would love, admire, support, and encourage me in the purpose for which You have called me.

Let me no longer manufacture my needs, and to fulfill them unnaturally; but as they were intended through love, through desire; through romance.

Where others see moments, let me see Opportunities. Where others see moments, let me make memories for them, to bring them closer to You. Let me catch the thoughts, the desires of my dreams, and manifest them in life before me. This is my prayer and desires of my heart this day Lord.

IJNAM

Printed in the USA
CPSIA information can be obtained
at www.ICGtesting.com
LVHW052044091224
798702LV00003B/4